T0095314

THE ADVENTURES OF RABBI ARIEH

A Destined Mission Around the World

Leo Michel Abrami

iUniverse, Inc.
New York   Bloomington

THE ADVENTURES OF RABBI ARIEH
A Destined Mission Around the World

iUniverse books may be ordered through booksellers or by contacting:

iUniverse
1663 Liberty Drive
Bloomington, IN 47403
www.iuniverse.com
1-800-Authors (1-800-288-4677)

ISBN: 978-1-4401-2182-1 (pbk)
ISBN: 978-1-4401-2184-5 (cloth)
ISBN: 978-1-4401-2183-8 (ebk)

Library of Congress Control Number: 2009922053

Printed in the United States of America

iUniverse rev. date: 3/9/2009

Contents

INTRODUCTION

"It is only in adventure that some people succeed in knowing themselves - in finding themselves" wrote Andre Gide, the 1947 Nobel Prize laureate for literature. I never doubted the truth of these words of wisdom. The hectic circumstances of my upbringing and the successive adventures of my professional career have surely helped me get a better understanding of myself. I still have to find myself.

I grew up in Bagnolet, a suburb of Paris, at a time of great upheaval. I was eight years old when the German army invaded France. Soon thereafter, the Nazis began the implementation of a regime of persecutions which affected the lives of Jews, Gypsies, homosexuals and communists. I witnessed the arrests of my Jewish friends who were deported to concentration camps. In 1942, we were compelled to wear a yellow star with the word Jew imprinted on it as if we were some specimen in a zoological garden. In order to avoid being caught by the German or French police, my mother arranged for me to live in the custody of a family of farmers in Normandy. I stayed on the farm for a year and a half. Even those who sheltered me did not know my true identity. I pretended I was a Catholic boy like all the other children. After the liberation of France by the Allies, I resumed a normal life and went back to school. When I was fifteen years old, I met a rabbi in Paris who took a special interest in me. When he suggested I enter a new section of the Jewish Theological seminary, I gladly accepted. Five years later, I became the cantor and religious school teacher of the *Grande Synagogue* of Geneva, Switzerland.

The impact of these experiences, however, never faded away. I always regarded myself as a survivor whose life was spared by some providential dispensation. After seven years of service to the Jewish community of Geneva, I pursued my vocation in the United States. I registered as a student at the Hebrew Union College in Cincinnati and I was ordained as a rabbi. I endeavored to bring the message of my faith to my people without paying much attention to the denominational affiliation of the particular congregation I served. I followed a *trans-denominational* - some would say *ecumenical* - approach to the Jewish religion. The term *ecumenical* is indeed appropriate since it is derived from the Biblical expression *Oikos Israel* which means the "House of Israel" in Greek.

During my career, I encountered the rigidity of the Orthodox rabbinate in all matters of Jewish law and the strong commitment of the Reform and Conservative movements to the changes they had enacted. I have been a member of four rabbinical associations and personally experienced the presumptuous character of their respective claims to authenticity. When I became a member of the Rabbinical Assembly of the Conservative movement, I was asked to resign my membership in the Central Conference of American Rabbis of the Reform movement. I reluctantly complied with the request. A year later, the Reform association re-instated me as a member of the Central Conference and I kept the two affiliations for several years until I resigned from both of them to become a *post-denominational* rabbi. My colleagues would often call me, in a facetious way, the *Refo-Conserva-Dox* or *Ortho-Conserva-Form* rabbi.

This approach has recently gained some acceptance in the Jewish community. Several non-denominational seminaries have been established in New York, Boston and Los Angeles, which are training rabbis who will be able to minister to the congregation of their choice if they are invited to do so. The main rabbinical organizations, however, still refuse to adopt such an open-minded approach because they fear that such a stand might undermine their *raison d'etre*. Each denomination still feels a need to uphold its ideological tenets and will not accept the principle of double allegiance. I was never able to accept these distinctions.

The Adventures of Rabbi Arieh describes the challenges which beset my career as a rabbi, mainly on account of my non-denominational and pluralistic attitude toward all segments of the Jewish community. My non-allegiance to one single denomination made my professional life more difficult but it was a matter of deep personal conviction. I have no regret at having pursued this idealistic goal. As Helen Keller once wrote: "Life is a daring adventure or nothing. To keep our faces toward change and behave like free spirits in the presence of fate is strength *undefeatable*."

All the facts and names mentioned in this book are true to the best of my recollection. I kindly ask for the indulgence of the reader for the errors which may have crept in my description of the events or the statements I reported in my account.

I am thankful to the Master of our Destinies for having given me the opportunity to be of service to the community of Israel and humanity. I am also grateful to all those who have helped me fulfill my vocation in the various parts of the world.

I wish to extend my deep appreciation to my wife Rosemary who kindly helped me with the preparation of this manuscript.

Leo Michel Abrami

Sun City West, Arizona

November 10. 2008

This volume is the sequel to another book, *Evading the Nazis, the Story of a Hidden Child in Normandy*, which was published in January 2009.

I

AT THE ONSET OF A TEACHING CAREER

When I told my friend Jack, a native of New York who was studying medicine at the University of Geneva, that I was making plans to attend a Rabbinical School in the United States, he laughed and said:

"You wouldn't believe it, Arieh. I had the same idea two years ago. When I told my father that I wanted to study for the rabbinate, he was not very happy. "Jack, my son," he said to me, "you should know that the rabbinate is not a profession for a nice Jewish boy like you; you should rather study medicine and be a doctor."

"And guess what happened?" he added with a smile, "I listened to my father. I applied for admission to five medical schools in the United States and as they wouldn't accept me, I applied to the school in Geneva and you know the rest of the story."

I might never have applied for admission to a seminary if unforeseen circumstances had not compelled me to make such a daring decision. I was twenty six years old and quite satisfied with my lot. I was the cantor of the *Grande Synagogue* of Geneva. My responsibilities included teaching in the Religious School and tutoring Bar Mitzvah students. I was studying child psychology and education at the *Institut Jean-Jacques Rousseau* on a part-time basis. During the preceding year, I had married Susan who was studying French literature at the university during her Junior year from Reed College in Oregon. We had just become the happy parents of a little girl. All seemed to go well for us when an unfortunate incident forced us to reconsider our plans for the future. It happened when my religious superior, the *Grand Rabbin* of Geneva, let me know, one morning, that he was dismayed by my demeanor in the community. He intimated to me that I would have to conform to his authority or resign from my post.

He was dissatisfied by the fact that my wife and I had become involved with a group of American, Canadian and British diplomats and functionaries who were working for the various agencies of the United Nations. These temporary residents of Geneva had formed the

English Speaking Jewish Congregation. Most of them, who belonged to Reform or Conservative congregations in their respective countries, were displeased by the fact that the synagogue services were conducted entirely in Hebrew and the women were not allowed to sit with their spouses in the sanctuary.

My wife and I had joined the group since its inception and we valued the company of our new friends. I was invited to teach a Sunday School class and prepare their boys and girls for their Bar/Bat Mitzvah celebration. The Chief Rabbi allowed the group to hold Sunday school classes in our Religious School building and agreed to let me teach in their school. When the time came for my first student to celebrate his Bar Mitzvah, the parents met with the rabbi to discuss the possibility of holding their own service in the synagogue, after the regular Sabbath morning service. The Chief Rabbi was willing to let the group conduct their service in Hebrew and English as they were accustomed, but he strongly objected to the principle of allowing men and women to sit together in the synagogue. This was contrary to Orthodox Jewish practice. Had the rabbi allowed the English-speaking group to have mixed seating in the synagogue for a Sabbath morning service, he would have been unable to uphold the Orthodox rule of gender separation, when his board of directors would approach him with a similar request.

As a consequence, the parents of the Bar Mitzvah made arrangements for the ceremony to take place in the Social Hall of the American Church of Geneva. The parents of the Bar Mitzvah invited me to participate in the service so that I might provide moral support to their son. We agreed that the service would begin at 11:15 am in order to allow me to walk from the synagogue to the church immediately after the traditional service was over.

On the day of the Bar Mitzvah, my wife and I walked swiftly to the American Church after the synagogue service and we joined a crowd of some two hundred attendees of all nationalities. We had a beautiful celebration which was marked by a fine participation and much singing on the part of all those present. The Bar Mitzvah chanted his Torah portion and delivered the sermon he had prepared with great assurance. The members of the family and the guests congratulated the Bar Mitzvah after the ceremony and I was proud of the fact that my student had done so well.

The next day, after we concluded the morning service in the chapel, the Chief Rabbi asked me to come to his office and he spoke to me with great severity:

"Monsieur Abrami, is it correct that you participated in the Bar Mitzvah celebration of the American boy at the Church yesterday?"

"Yes, Rabbi," I replied. "I did it because I taught him his Torah portion and some of the prayers and he wanted me to be near him during the service so that I might assist him in case he needed help."

The Chief Rabbi then said:

"Monsieur Abrami, you cannot pursue this kind of activity. You must decide which congregation you want to serve, theirs or ours, but you cannot continue to officiate in the two congregations at the same time."

"Yes, Rabbi, I understand what you mean. I will make the decision in the next few days and I will let you know."

That was not an easy decision to make. After seven years of devoted service to the community, I had come to regard the members of the congregation as part of my extended family and Geneva as my home. I was beginning to make an impact on some of my students and I regretted having to leave them. At the same time, however, I now felt the need to pursue my religious studies in a liberal seminary. For the past seven years, I had often questioned the wisdom of some of the decisions which were made by my superior. After reflection, my wife and I decided to go to the United States where I would study in a liberal seminary since there was no such school in Europe at the time. I was eager to get acquainted with the various religious expressions which obtained in the American Jewish community. I therefore applied for admission to two seminaries in the United States, the Jewish Theological Seminary in New York City, which trained Conservative rabbis, and the Hebrew Union College, Cincinnati, the most important Reform seminary in the world. The New York seminary requested that I come to the United States to be examined so that they might determine whether to accept me or not. The Hebrew Union College followed a different procedure. They suggested that I be interviewed by one of their professors, Dr. Julius Levy, who happened to be on a sabbatical leave in Europe at the time. Five weeks after I applied for admission, I received a letter of acceptance from the Hebrew Union College. I was also granted a tuition scholarship which stipulated that I would have to serve one of the congregations affiliated with the World Union of Progressive Judaism for three years after my ordination as a rabbi. Since my wife and I were planning to return to Europe, I accepted the condition without hesitation.

We sold or gave away whatever we possessed. I passed an aptitude test in the English language at the American Consulate and I obtained a student visa. The Consul General, who was a member of the new congregation, invited us to his home to meet his family before we left Geneva. The Chief Rabbi considered my decision to study at a liberal seminary as an act of defection from traditional Judaism and the board members stood by him even though the majority were by no means Orthodox Jews. Several of them were intermarried and quite assimilated. They did not attend the farewell reception a group of friends organized for me and my family on the day before we departed from Geneva. I was now on my way to one of the great adventures of my life.

The English Speaking Jewish Congregation led to the formation of a Liberal congregation for the entire community and it is today the most dynamic Jewish association in Geneva.

II

THE HEBREW UNION COLLEGE

My wife, our daughter and I left Switzerland for the United States via Amsterdam and San Francisco and we arrived in Cincinnati in August 1960. We found a suitable apartment in Avondale, a racially mixed neighborhood some fifteen minutes away from the Hebrew Union College. As in many other American cities, the white middle class residents were in the process of moving toward the suburbs, leaving behind their houses, their commercial centers and their places of worship. As a consequence, one could see large realty signs displayed all over this part of the city. In Cincinnati and Avondale, there were three synagogues for sale and no buyer.

The college was located on a large campus in one of the most desirable parts of the city. The University of Cincinnati was right across the avenue. The institution bore no resemblance to the Paris seminary where I had studied. It looked more like a university than a traditional Yeshivah. Surpassing in height all the other buildings, was the newest and finest library of Judaica and related books in the whole world, containing over a million volumes and many original manuscripts and *incunabula*. This institution reflected the aspirations of the pioneers of the Reform movement who were convinced that the academic study of the Jewish religion would facilitate a reconciliation between the conceptions of modern science and philosophy and the perennial teachings of the Jewish religion.

A few days before the beginning of the fall session, I was tested on my knowledge of Hebrew and Bible and allowed to attend the third year classes in the rabbinical program of the college. I could easily follow the lectures in English, but I wrote most of my assignments in French and my professors were quite courteous about it.

There were thirty students in my class who had come from various parts of the country and a few from abroad. Each of them had a different religious background and a different reason for wanting to become a rabbi. A few felt that they had to fulfill their spiritual vocation to serve God and humanity with all their heart, others were hoping to become teachers and preachers of the Jewish tradition in order to perpetuate the teachings of Judaism. Virtually all of them were primarily motivated to become successful leaders of the Jewish community. Consequently, the communal and social aspects of the rabbinical profession often took precedence over the philosophical and spiritual ones. Many students were more inclined to study subjects like human relations, personal counseling, temple administration, educational policies and ways of promoting social justice in the community at large than in biblical archeology or medieval philosophy. The curriculum of studies was probably conceived to meet these needs.

Our daily program of activities included a short prayer service at 10:45 in mid-morning. Some of my classmates and I, who had come from abroad, were not accustomed to such a practice and we decided to have our own traditional prayer service early in the morning. Since it was our intention to dedicate our lives to God and the Jewish religion, we felt that we ought to begin each day with a prayer service before we went to our respective classes. We were five in our prayer group; we prayed in Hebrew and donned our *Tallit* (prayer shawl) and our *Tefilin* (phylacteries) as some of us were wont to do before we came to the college.

A week after we had started our morning small *minyan,* I was called to the office of Dr. Sheldon Blank, our professor of biblical studies. His responsibilities included the supervision of all services held in the chapel of the college. He spoke to me with great seriousness:

"Leo, or should I say Arieh, it has come to my attention that you have organized a traditional prayer service in the morning with phylacteries. You know, Leo, we do not do these things in America. You should learn the American way and do what we are doing at the college."

I was surprised by the tone of these remarks but I did not try to engage in a discussion in my deficient English. Conscious of the fact that I was only a student who had just arrived from Europe, I agreed to discontinue our *minyan* in the chapel. I would pray alone in my apartment before going to the college. I did not understand, however, why a distinguished professor in a liberal institution was opposed to a practice which had been observed with reverence for centuries. I resolved to contain my feelings of disappointment and I engaged in my studies with all my being.

Dr. Blank was not the only professor who held this attitude toward tradition. Several other members of the faculty would chastise traditional customs on occasion. They thought that these were contrary to the principles of Reform Judaism and were not compatible with the American way of life. Since most Americans are wont to attend one religious service every week, they probably felt that they should emulate that custom. It was indeed more convenient to attend one late service on Friday night than participate in two or more services every week. Most of my classmates had no difficulties following the American way but I was not ready at this stage to abandon the practice of traditional daily prayer, the wearing of a prayer-shawl or the donning of phylacteries.

One of the most severe critics of orthodoxy was Dr. Alvin Reines, our professor of Jewish religious thought. He taught with great passion, often pointing out the inconsistencies of certain traditional beliefs. Even the accepted doctrine of *ethical monotheism*, which was regarded as one of the fundamental teachings of Reform Judaism, was not immune to his critical examination. He could not accept the basic premise of *theism*, the belief in a personal God watching over the destinies of

His creatures. For a whole trimester, we studied a text-
book which presented the notion of a finite God who
had only limited power to do what He would have liked
to do. I felt personally hurt by such a lack of reverence
for the teachings of the Biblical prophets, let alone the
theological doctrines of the early pioneers of the Reform
movement.

As he was approaching the age of retirement, the
professor's attitude toward the teachings of Judaism
became clear. He declared himself to be a humanist,
in other terms, an agnostic. He had lost his faith in
God while he was still a young man. Instead of calling
himself an agnostic, however, he preferred to use a more
sophisticated and ethereal term to describe his attitude
toward religion. He called himself an adept of *polydox*
Judaism, a neologism he had invented to mask his non-
belief in a supreme being, without offending too many
people.

One of my classmates who adhered to his philosophy,
became convinced that the teachings of Reform Judaism
were compatible with those of the Unitarian-Universalist
Church. He became the week-end acting minister of
one of their churches. There was little objection on the
part of the faculty of the college and some professors

thought it was actually a significant achievement in the field of interfaith relations.

I experienced another dilemma with respect to the attitude of several professors toward Zionism and the State of Israel. A majority of the leaders of the Reform movement had wholeheartedly welcomed the establishment of the State of Israel some twelve years before, but others were still ambivalent about the creation of the state. Some were adamantly opposed to the very notion of the existence of an autonomous Jewish state. They were ostensibly afraid that any support for a foreign state might lead some American citizens to question their loyalty to the United States. At the time, many of them joined the American Council for Judaism, an organization which was openly opposed to the existence of the Israeli state. I just could not understand the negative attitude of so many Reform rabbis toward the State of Israel. I was wondering why they were dissociating themselves from the plight of the European and Mediterranean survivors of the Holocaust and their attempt to start a new life in the land of their ancestors.

In the course of time, the American Reform movement progressively changed its attitude toward

Israel and it eventually became one of its staunchest supporters. Under the leadership of Professor Nelson Gluck, the president of the college, a branch of the Hebrew Union College was established in Jerusalem. The movement decided to assist in the creation of a number of congregations in various parts of Israel. It also sponsored the establishment of two collective farms (*Kibbutzim*) in the southern part of the country. The Reform movement is now participating in the development of the Holy land in more than one way. It has also made a determined effort to recapture many of the customs and rituals it had previously discarded and a new spirit of reverence for tradition seems to prevail today in the ranks of the movement.

There were two professors with whom I established a warm and friendly relation. Both were natives of Europe where they were nurtured by traditional Judaism. One of them was Dr Jacob Petuchowski, who had been a private student in London of Rabbi Leo Baeck, the president of the World Union for Progressive Judaism and a former rabbi of Berlin. The other was Dr Alexander Guttmann, a former professor at the Breslau Rabbinical Seminary, who taught Talmud and codes. Dr Petuchowski became my mentor during the three years I spent at the college.

He had encountered problems with his colleagues in his first years as an assistant professor. They had objected to the fact that his approach to Judaism did not coincide with theirs. He was compelled to leave the faculty but he was later reinstated after the intervention of a prominent member of the College Board of Directors. All these facts led me to believe that even in the most liberal seminary in the world, ideological differences were not always well tolerated. When I shared my concerns with Dr. Petuchowski, he answered me candidly:

"I must tell you, Arieh, that you are not the only one to experience reservations about the mainstream ideology of the Reform movement. Other students have experienced difficulties too and have managed to succeed in the rabbinate in spite of them. So be patient and try to set aside these frustrations, at least, temporarily."

He explained to me that the American movement was different from its European counterpart in many respects and that was probably the cause of my disappointment with the college.

"When you return to Europe," he said to me, "these problems will have vanished and you will have to face other ones. You must bear in mind, Arieh, that wherever you go, you will encounter new situations and be confronted by new challenges which will require that you be forbearing for a time. I suggest that you complete your studies first and decide later what particular approach to Judaism you will embrace."

These were indeed words of wisdom but they did not alleviate the frustrations I was experiencing at the time. I endeavored to follow the advice of my professor and I pursued my studies with assiduity. I found many areas of special interest to sustain my passion for knowledge. I signed up for several elective seminars, including one devoted to the study of Maimonides' *Guide for the Perplexed* which was given by Dr. Reines. Strangely enough, it was one of the finest seminars I attended at the college. It was probably due to the fact that he was often quoting from the notes he had taken in the classes of Professor Harry A. Wolfson at Harvard University during the years he spent there studying for his doctorate. He was a fine teacher, albeit not a believer in an immanent and transcendent God. In a paradoxical way, his teachings strengthened my faith in a personal God.

In the course of my readings in the library, I discovered that there were various progressive movements which were developing in the American Jewish community in addition to the Reform movement. I decided to investigate them and find out more about the respective ideologies they were advocating. I made arrangements to attend the conference of the Reconstructionist Foundation which was held in Chicago in mid-winter. The founder of the movement, Rabbi Mordecai Kaplan, made a profound impression on me. The elderly professor with white hair and a white beard inspired reverence. He had taught homiletics at the Jewish Theological Seminary in New York for over fifty years until he retired. He was now devoting himself entirely to the writing of books and essays which were meant to clarify his approach to Judaism. He would describe himself as a religious humanist, a naturalist and a pragmatist going so far as to borrow the word *Reconstructionism* from the title of a book of his teacher and friend, Columbia University professor John Dewey. The latter was one of the great proponents of the pragmatist school of philosophy.

In the light of this knowledge, Kaplan formulated a concise definition of the Jewish religion. *"Judaism,"* he asserted, *"is the evolving religious civilization of the Jewish people"* thus combining the ethnic, social, cultural and spiritual aspects of the heritage of the Jewish people.

His main book, *Judaism as a civilization,* served as a guide for the new Reconstructionist movement.

I was particularly moved by one of his interventions during the conference. In a session which dealt with the need to modernize the Ketubah, the traditional marriage certificate, Rabbi Kaplan took a stand that was most thoughtful and conciliatory, even though it did not solve the problem entirely. After some of the young rabbis of the movement moved to abandon the text of the old document and replace it with a more relevant one which would reflect contemporary concerns, he took the floor and with great composure and tact, addressed the participants in these words:

"My friends, I do not think we ought to abandon the traditional Ketubah. You see, this marriage certificate has been used for centuries by our people, and we cannot discard it with a stroke of the hand. I would like to propose that we join the two texts together, the traditional and the contemporary texts, so that we might be constantly reminded that ours is *an evolving religious civilization.*"

A few years later, the Rabbinical Assembly of Conservative Judaism adopted a new marriage certificate in the form of a *triptique* certificate, which contained three columns, one with the traditional Ketubah in its original Aramaic, one that had a modern rendition in Hebrew and one containing an English translation of the latter. The rabbis justified their decision by asserting that it was done according to the accepted dialectic of *tradition and change* advocated by the Conservative movement.

Pursuing my readings in the library, I discovered the works of another outstanding religious thinker who had actually taught at the College during the war years. Indeed, Dr Abraham Joshua Heschel had been invited to join the faculty of the College. He was granted an affidavit to come to America, just a few weeks before the Germans decided to put an end to all emigration from Germany. After completing his five year contract at the College, Dr Heschel was invited to teach at the Jewish Theological Seminary in New York. During his career, he published a number of important books and distinguished himself as an eminent advocate for human rights in the United States. He was one of the few rabbis who marched at the side of Rev. Martin Luther King Jr. in the memorable manifestation of solidarity with the black community which took place in Salem, Alabama. His writings spoke to my heart and I became a silent disciple of his. At the College, his name was barely mentioned. One of the professors had labeled him a *rhetorician of faith* and not a true philosopher. Whether rhetorician or philosopher, however, his writings and his exemplary conduct provided the moral and spiritual support I needed to go on and finish my studies at the college.

After several months of exposure to his ideas, I decided to fly to New York to meet him personally. I was privileged to have two long conversations with him in his home on Riverside Drive. Each time I asked him to comment upon a given topic, he would answer me briefly and ask me to tell him about the college. He was eager to know what was going on at the school where he had taught for five years

Besides the basic disciplines like Bible, Talmud, religious philosophy and liturgy, the curriculum of studies included several subjects of particular relevance to the career of a modern rabbi. Among them was a course in Jewish education mainly concerned with teaching methods and curriculum which was taught by Dr. Sylvan Schwarzman. In addition to these courses, he also taught a *practicum* in the rabbinical profession to the fifth year students. One of the sessions, which was part of this course, was devoted to the way a young rabbi should conduct himself in an interview with a rabbi's search committee. He suggested that we always use common sense and deal with the practical aspects of the rabbinical profession rather than the philosophical or theological ones and if asked by a committee member the delicate question:

"Rabbi, let us now consider some of the financial aspects of your service to our congregation; in the event we were to engage you as our rabbi, what kind of remuneration would you expect?"

To such a question, suggested the professor, you might answer this way,

"Ladies and gentlemen, if I am to reside and work in this community, I would like to be able to live the way most of you live."

He then predicted that there would be a brief moment of silence because the committee members could not have expected so much boldness on the part of a rabbi, still considered by many as an employee of the synagogue. The treasurer or some other member of the committee who would have understood the humor involved in this repartee, would probably restate the question and say,

"Rabbi, let's be more practical; please give us a figure."

We all laughed as we recognized the ingenuity of the interviewing process he was suggesting to us.

Our professor of human relations, Dr Robert Katz, taught us how to establish good relations with the members of our congregation and use the proper methods of achieving change in a communal setting. The curriculum of one of his courses included the study of several manuals on social change and essays by Kurt Levine which dealt with the psychological ways of effecting change in a group. He was particularly keen in teaching us the difference that exists between *sympathy* and *empathy*.

"When you are engaged in a counseling session," he said in one of his classes, "you must focus all your attention on your counselee and never say words like 'I know how you feel, I was in the same situation once' and then continue telling your story instead of listening to the person who came to you for psychological or spiritual guidance."

Dr Katz later published a fine book entitled *Empathic Process and Religious Counseling* which has since become required study in the training of pastoral counselors at many universities and seminaries. He would use inter-active techniques like the method of psychodrama of Prof. Jacob Levy Moreno, to make us sensitive to the impact we have on others and others have on us. He would often invite lecturers to address us on major contemporary issues. When he heard that the distinguished Professor Viktor Frankl from Vienna, Austria had been invited to give a series of lectures at the University of Cincinnati, he immediately invited him to the college too.

Frankl gave us five lectures which had a profound impact on me. He was a survivor of the concentration camps where his parents and his wife were murdered. After the war, he was appointed professor of neurology and psychiatry at the medical school of the University of Vienna, Austria. He presented to us the main principles of his new approach to psychotherapy which is centered on the meaning of life. First referred to as *existential analysis,* he later called it *logotherapy,* a neologism derived from the Greek word *logos*, which means word or meaning. I began to read Frankl's books with great eagerness. A few years later, I pursued my studies at the Institute of Logotherapy of Berkeley, California. I wrote a number of essays and a systematic introduction in

French *Une Démarche Thérapeutique: la Logothérapie* (a therapeutic method: logotherapy) which was published in Paris in 2006.

Disciplines like mysticism and Kabbalah were not part of our program of studies. The founders of the Reform movement regarded these subjects with great suspicion. They believed they were not compatible with the rational and historical approach to the study of religion. The historian Heinrich Graetz, among others, had severely criticized Kabbalah in his writings and had gone so far as to advance the view that it did not belong to the core of the Jewish religion. It would seem, however, that even such a strong opposition to mysticism has been overcome in the last few years. The college curriculum of studies has been overhauled several times in the last decades and it includes today many disciplines which were never taught before.

When I decided to write my master's thesis on the allegorical and mystical interpretations of the biblical book of Song of Songs, I could not find a professor who would guide me, but realizing how much it meant to me, Dr Petuchowski agreed to be the faculty member who would supervise the writing of my thesis. I still remember the private conversation we had at the time.

"Arieh, I am not an expert in that field, but I am willing to give you some guidance with respect to methodology. You will have to pursue your own research and write your thesis with little assistance from me."

He actually helped me a great deal in my research. Without the moral support I received from him, I would never have been able to pursue my studies at the college.

In the fall season, just before the school year began, my wife and I were happy to welcome Dan, our second child and first son. He was born at St Mary's Hospital which was adjacent to the college. I had to make a special request and instruct the doctors to save the mother first and then the child in case a grave problem were to occur during the delivery and a difficult choice had to be made. At the time, the code of medical ethics of St Mary's Hospital stipulated that in such a case, the doctors were to save the child first and then the mother so that the child might be baptized according to Catholic teachings. Since that time, however, the prelates of the Roman Catholic Church have modified this canonic law.

In order to enable the students to get some practical experience, the college had arranged a whole program of partial internships. The students were given the opportunity to serve small congregations on week-ends or on a biweekly basis and during the High Holidays. As soon as I arrived in the United States, I was invited to conduct services in Rapid City, South Dakota for the members of a small congregation who met only twice a year for the High Holidays. Even though I was still struggling with the English language, the members of the congregation treated me with great courtesy and kindness. The president called for me at the airport and took me right away to a luncheon-meeting of the International Club. I was invited to speak about the political situation in France and the government of Charles De Gaulle, immediately after an address by U.S. Senator Mc Govern. I had never shared such an honor in my life before.

We conducted our services in the military chapel of a near-by Air-force base. I spent the eight days between Rosh Hashanah and Yom Kippur meeting with various members of the congregation. They were all eager to discuss some of their personal problems with me and I did my best to counsel them.

The following year, I was invited to serve as the cantor in a small congregation in Kokomo, Indiana with a fifth year rabbinical student who served as the acting rabbi. He read the prayers in English and delivered the sermons and I chanted the traditional liturgy in Hebrew. We worked as a team until five o'clock in the afternoon of Yom Kippur. My colleague then said to me:

"Arieh, I am tired, let's finish the service."

He then turned to the last page of our prayer-book, and concluded the service, even though the sun was still shining through the stained glass windows of the synagogue. The members of the congregation were quite embarrassed, but there was little they could do after he had blown the Shofar to mark the end of the holy day. We went to the Social Hall in order to break the fast but nothing was ready, because the volunteers did not expect the service to end before night fall, two hours later. So the president of the congregation turned to me and asked me to sing a few songs to allow the sisterhood ladies to prepare the food. I agreed to his request and I went on singing until it got completely dark. We then celebrated the *Havdalah* to mark the end of the Day of Atonement and proceeded with our break-the-fast collation. It was quite a moving experience for all of us, except for my colleague who did not try to justify his decision to end the service in the middle of the afternoon. We then returned to our respective families in Cincinnati.

On Friday nights, I would attend services in the chapel of the college, I was invited to join the choir and I would sing a few solos from time to time. On Saturday mornings, I would often go with a Japanese classmate of mine, Hiroshi Okamoto, to a little Orthodox synagogue where the rabbi would read the entire Torah portion of the week instead of the eight or ten verses which were read at the college.

In order to further develop my teaching experience, I accepted a part-time position as a Hebrew teacher in the religious school of Congregation Adath Israel which was the leading Conservative congregation in Cincinnati. Rabbi Newman, who was the school principal, was a very conscientious and dedicated educator. In order to ensure the quality of the teaching which was provided by his school, he had installed in every classroom, a sophisticated system of microphones and loudspeakers which would enable him to listen in to what was going on in every class. One evening, after I finished my class, he let me know that I should come to his office because he wanted to talk to me.

"Arieh," he said, "your Hebrew teaching is fine and the children enjoy your classes, but a group of parents came to see me a few days ago, and they expressed to me a specific concern. They think that you are referring to the holocaust too often in your classes and they have asked me to let you know that they do not want their children to learn about the persecutions and the atrocities of World War II. Please take this advice into account."

"Rabbi," I said, "I cannot understand these parents: they are asking me to remain silent about one of the worst tragedies which befell our people. Do they think that their children will be more happy if they don't learn about the destruction of entire European Jewish communities?"

"Arieh," he replied,"I personally agree with you; I am only conveying to you the feelings of several parents."

"Then," I said, "I will spend more time talking to the parents at the end of the class."

"This may, indeed, be the best way of avoiding criticism," said the rabbi.

At the beginning of the next academic year, new faces appeared on the campus. One of the new students enrolled in the doctoral program was from the city of Montreal. He was a member of the Jesuit order who had not yet been ordained as a priest. We were immediately attracted to each other on account of our linguistic and cultural affinity. We spent much time together discussing the matters we were studying in our respective classes and many topics of mutual interest. He was open-minded and willing to learn about doctrines and concepts which were different from his own. We respected each other's beliefs in a good *ecumenical* spirit. Only once did his convictions give way to an expression of faith that he was unable to control. He told me:

"If you believe in the divine inspiration of Scriptures, why can't you believe that the New Testament is equally inspired?"

The moment he had finished stating his question, however, he realized he had trespassed one of the unspoken rules we were both abiding by and we did not pursue that topic. We never let our different religious beliefs interfere with our friendship. Jean Ouelette eventually completed his studies and received a Ph.D. degree from the college. He left the Jesuit order to devote himself to archeological research in Israel for several years. He later accepted to teach Judaic Studies at Concordia University and then, at the *Université de*

Montréal. In due time, Jean married an Israeli woman and he became the father of three children. He has become a strong advocate for the State of Israel and is a member of the executive committee of the Canadian Institute for Jewish Research. One of his sons works full-time for the institute. We met again forty five years later and we re-kindled our friendship which now includes the members of our families.

As I began to think about what I might do after graduation, I made an appointment to see Dr. Martin Cohen, the dean of students, to discuss my future with him. I told him that I would like to return to France, but if I could not do so, I would consider spending two years in the Soviet Union to be of service to the Jewish community in some capacity. I would either teach at some university or do some social work within the Jewish community if government regulations did not permit me to assume a rabbinical post. He smiled and he said:

"Arieh, you must be dreaming. There is not a chance that you would be able to do these things in the Soviet Union at this time. You should be more practical and consider some tangible possibilities in the free world."

I was very disappointed by the fact that he had simply dismissed my suggestion and called it a dream. It did look like a dream, but it was not a fantasy altogether. Elie Wiesel and other activists of the movement for Soviet Jewry were beginning to draw our attention to the plight of our Russian brethren. A few academics and other visitors had made contacts with various groups of Soviet Jews and they all reported that our Russian brothers were eager to learn about their heritage, a privilege which had been denied them for several generations. I came to the conclusion that I had spoken to the wrong person. Dr. Cohen was a distinguished historian of the past but he could not visualize the future.

I was deeply convinced that my services would be most needed in the country of my birth. Several hundred thousand coreligionists had just arrived in France after they were expelled from Algeria the moment the country proclaimed its independence. I was looking forward to create a model congregation patterned on some of the most creative ways which had been developed in the United States. I was also hoping that my newly acquired knowledge of some aspects of the Jewish heritage would give me the ability to attract many new members.

I completed the course work of the third and fourth year of rabbinical studies in two years and I began writing my master's thesis which marks the completion of the rabbinical studies. I was then informed that I had to take many of the first and second year courses in order to graduate. I reluctantly agreed to do so in order to fulfill the requirements. I passed the examination for the Baccalaureate in Hebrew Letters with honors and fulfilled the requirements for the master's degree at the same time. I was ordained as a rabbi three years after I enrolled at the college. The ceremony took place in the old Reform Temple on Plum Street in Cincinnati, which was closed all year long, except on special occasions.

I was now looking forward to returning to France in order to minister to one of the new communities which were mushrooming all over the country. I was told, however, that there had been no formal request for a liberal rabbi in France. They suggested I go to England or Guatemala in order to fulfill my requirement to serve a congregation of the World Union for Progressive Judaism. I was extremely disappointed by this turn of events and was deeply grieved by it. I now had to set aside my dream of returning to my country and after a short stay in England, I accepted the Guatemala-City position.

I regretted the fact that the World Union did not take advantage of my knowledge of the French language, its culture and country, to send me to France. I might have lent assistance to the new immigrants who were arriving in droves. I pleaded with the organization to no avail. I came to the conclusion that rabbis sitting at comfortable desks in a New York office behave like bureaucrats anywhere in the world. The director of the World Union advised me to accept the post in Guatemala so that he might comply with the request he had received from a group of some three dozen families in Guatemala-City. He was now able to stick a little flag on the world map that was hanging in his office. In the mean time, I and my family quite reluctantly went to a distant country to minister to a small group of people who spoke a language I did not even understand.

III

A RABBI IN MAYAN COUNTRY

Guatemala-City was unlike any city I had visited before. It was built at an altitude of some five thousand feet above sea level, near two great volcanoes which were not completely extinct. One could still see, from time to time, some small flames billowing into the sky at night from the Fuego (fire) volcano. The trees were blooming and filling the air with a sweet fragrance. Some of the residential suburbs had been built in recent years and the large and lavish houses indicated the level of affluence of those who lived in them. Every residence was built around an interior courtyard in a Spanish style, which always included a quarter for the servants. The downtown area, however, was crowded and noisy. One could barely breathe the air which was heavily polluted with the exhaust gases of old diesel buses that had not been properly serviced in years.

A few crypto-Jews had settled in the country in the period that followed the *Conquista* by the Spaniards in the sixteenth century. When some of them attempted to return to Judaism and practice their faith openly, the Church established a Tribunal of the Inquisition in the land. Its agents arrested the lapsed *new-Christians* who had been accused of secretly practicing Judaism and they were sentenced to various prison terms and some to die at the stake. The Crypto-Jews eventually vanished from existence a century later. In the middle of the nineteenth century, a small contingent of German Jews arrived in the country together with a larger group of German immigrants. They too assimilated in less than two or three generations and practically disappeared. Then, in the aftermath of the First World War, some fifty families from Syria and Lebanon settled in the country. They were followed a generation later by several groups of refugees from Germany, Poland and Hungary who arrived just before or after World War II.

In 1964, there were four congregations in Guatemala-City for a Jewish population of a little over one thousand individuals. Each ethnic group was eager to assert its cultural and religious identity and refused to merge with the others. They formed a joint committee only when there was a need to fight anti-Semitism and to support the State of Israel. The Jews from the Middle East built a synagogue in the down-town area. The members of the Polish and Hungarian congregation started building a synagogue in a residential suburb of the city but it remained unfinished for many years. They would conduct their services in the portion of the building which was covered with a roof. The German group prayed in the home of one of their members in the downtown area. They would have an early traditional service on Saturday morning which would be concluded before 9:00 am so that they might be able to open their stores after the service.

There was now a new generation of Jews who were for the most part born in the country and whose mother-tongue was Spanish and no more Judeo-Arabic, German or Yiddish and they decided to form their own congregation opting for the Reform ideology. They were young couples who had virtually no memories of the European or Middle Eastern communities from which their parents had originated. They considered themselves to be full-fledged Guatemalan citizens and were determined proudly to assert their new identity.

On account of the pressures of their professional occupations, the members of my congregation had decided that they would hold only a Friday night service. As a result, I felt quite frustrated because I had never missed a Saturday morning service in my life. I discussed the matter with the president of the congregation who told me that if I felt an irresistible urge to attend a Sabbath morning service, I could do so at one of the other synagogues. The members of my congregation were under the impression that Reform Judaism did not demand so much devotion and that a religious gathering once a week should have been quite sufficient.

I gave a number of lecture-sermons on various topics in order to attract members and visitors to our services but I was not prepared to conduct a symbolic Torah service on Friday nights as was done in many Reform congregations in the United States. We would have an interactive Torah study session in lieu of the formal reading in the scroll. On Saturday morning, I began to attend services at the other synagogues and I became acquainted with all the Jews of the city. After a few months, they invited me to participate in their services. When the Torah reader of the German group fell ill, I was asked if I would read the entire Torah portion of the week and I accepted gladly. When I attended services at the Polish congregation, they would often invite me to give a commentary on the Torah portion or the *Haftarah* (prophetic reading) of the week and conduct a part of the service. I prepared a few boys from the Sephardic congregation to be Bar Mitzvah and the ceremony took place at their synagogue. On these occasions, the president of the congregation would invite me to give the sermon. For all practical purposes, I had become a community rabbi in this isolated Jewish community of Central America.

The members of my congregation were very displeased with my activities. They would have liked to stop me from getting involved with the other congregations. They had hired me in an attempt to separate themselves from the other Jewish groups of the city and not to cooperate with them. They called the head office of the World Union for Progressive Judaism in New York to complain about my activities in the community, but they were unable to sway its director to pressure me on this matter. They were told that if they were dissatisfied with my services, they could terminate my services but that the reputation of the congregation might be damaged by such a decision. In addition, the World Union might not be able to find another rabbi to agree to go to Guatemala. After further reflection, the members of my board of directors realized that there was actually an advantage to my getting involved with the other congregations. It would thus prove that Reform Judaism was not a sectarian movement as many believed at first, but a new expression of the Jewish religion that was concerned with the welfare of the entire community as a whole. After a few months, a number of prominent members of the other groups eventually joined our congregation though some of them still maintained their affiliation with their former congregation. My efforts to reach out to the community at large had been vindicated and I thought I had proven the validity of my approach to communal matters when I was confronted with another problem.

A couple came to see me one day and asked me to perform their marriage. The groom was Jewish but his fiancée was Catholic. I explained to them that I would only perform the ceremony if the bride were to consider the possibility of converting to Judaism. At that moment, the groom did not wait for his bride to answer and he replied for her that this was out of the question. I then said that it would be a relatively simple matter and that he should call me if he thought his bride might be willing to undertake the study of Judaism. He never called me back. I later learned from a member of my congregation that he had expected that answer on my part and that he had made an appointment on that same day to meet with a Catholic priest, who eventually agreed to officiate at their marriage in the Church, after he converted to Catholicism. I was very sad and torn inside about this episode and I promised myself that I would endeavor to find a better approach to avoid being confronted with a similar situation in the future. I eventually conceived a list of pertinent questions I would ask the couple about their personal religious convictions. We would then engage in a dialogue which would often give me a chance to say with a tinge of humor:

"My friend, you have proven to me that your religious convictions are closer to that of Judaism than to any other religion. You are definitely more Jewish than you thought."

The couple would then feel more inclined to pursue the Jewish way. I would then prepare the non-Jewish partner for conversion. The members of my congregation did not understand my attitude on this matter. They had been told that Reform rabbis were quite lenient on intermarriage and they expected me to perform marriages between Jews and Gentiles as was widely done in American Reform congregations.

My wife and children all learned to read and speak Spanish in a few months. I registered for an intensive course at the American Cultural Center and made rapid progress in my ability to speak and write the language. A member of my congregation who was a high school teacher, helped me translate my sermons and lectures into Spanish and I was soon able to take an active part in the various aspects of the social and cultural life of the community at large.

I began to understand some of the characteristics of the Latin American way of life. This initiation was facilitated by various contacts I had with members of the local government. Indeed, one of the United States Embassy attachés, and a member of my congregation, invited me to join a small informal group of American and Guatemalan diplomats and civil servants which met once a month in a down-town restaurant in order to discuss matters of common interest. The opinions of our Latin American friends were quite enlightening.

On one occasion, a Guatemalan participant focused our attention on the right that politicians and civil servants have to invite members of their family and friends to assume government posts because they are in a position to do so. In other terms, he felt that the practice, which is often called *nepotism* and is usually regarded as unethical in the Western world, was perfectly legitimate in Latin America.

"If you can help a relative or a friend,' said the Guatemalan civil servant, "why wouldn't you do it?" and most of his colleagues agreed with him. After several discussions on that theme, the American members of our group conceded that they had not succeeded in convincing their Latin colleagues that it was morally wrong to do so. The Guatemalan members of our group were strongly maintaining that it was an honored practice in their country and in the rest of the Latin-American continent as a whole.

A few months later, the cultural attaché of the embassy asked me to contact the director of the Ministry of Urban Development who had a question I might be able to answer. I called him and he told me on the phone that he was eager to talk to me about Jewish methods of meditation. I agreed to meet him in his office at the ministry. We had a friendly conversation during which I told him everything I knew about meditation and I then asked him why he was interested in the subject. He told me that he had tried various methods in the past year in order to find a remedy for his insomnia, but none of them had been helpful to him so far. I asked him why he could not fall asleep and there was a moment of silence and after eight or ten seconds, he resolved to speak and he explained to me the reason.

"The answer to that question," he said to me, "is connected to my work."

He stood up and invited me to follow him.

"You see," he said, "in all these cabinets and these closets, you will find the blue- prints of many original projects my staff and I have been working on for the past ten years. We made extensive plans for the urban development of several cities, we conceived original projects which included the creation of entire new neighborhoods with schools and post office and everything you might need in a new suburb of a city. I designed all these plans in accordance to the best norms of modern urbanism they taught me at Cornell University."

"And what happened to all these projects?" I asked.

"I must tell you with great chagrin," he answered, "that I have not seen, as yet, any of them become a reality. My colleagues and I often work on a project for several months; we prepare blue-prints, we draw the architect's impressions and we have them bound in a book form. I then bring a few copies of the particular project to the minister in charge of Urban Development, who in turn gives two copies to the president of the state."

"Is it not the usual procedure in most countries?" I asked.

"No," he said, "because in our case, the president or a member of the cabinet takes these blue-prints and flies to Washington, DC. He arranges for a meeting with a representative of the *Alliance for Progress* of the American government. He hands over the two copies of my project to the director of that agency and he then requests a grant which would permit the realization of the project. By some chance, he will obtain a substantial grant. The check is then deposited in an overseas bank and the bulk of the money may seldom reach our country. As you can see, I produced many blue-prints, but they have not been implemented as yet. That is the sad story of my life."

I was overwhelmed by the strong emotions of this man and I wanted to share my sympathy with him.

"I deeply admire your devotion to the welfare of your country," I said. "If I were in the same predicament, I would probably not be able to sleep at night either."

Feeling the need to be more comforting, however, I said to him:

"You are a good man, Señor. You are trying to improve the living conditions of your people to the best of your abilities. In truth, your devotion must be accounted as the finest offering a man can present to the Creator."

I wish I had been able to help this man overcome his problem with the authorities but all I could do was to alleviate some of his anxiety by extending my sympathy to him.

The general who had seized power in the country was not able to control the terrorist activities of the guerillas who were operating in several provinces and even in the capital. Supported by the Fidel Castro regime, these fighters were attempting to undermine the authority of the government and hoping that an uprising might bring about a revolutionary regime on the model of the Cuban one.

One evening, as our American friends were taking us back home in a car that carried embassy plates, we had a frightening encounter with these terrorists. A station wagon had just passed us when it suddenly slowed down right in front of us forcing us to swerve to the right in order to avoid a collision. A man with a powerful torch in the front seat and another in the back seat with a machine-gun quickly checked each one of us and let us continue our way. We were not the targeted victims they had planned to murder that night. We reported the incident to the military police the next day. Within a few months, however, the American ambassador and then, the German ambassador were both murdered in similar ambushes.

A leading member of the Jewish community who was in his early eighties, was abducted in the downtown area of Guatemala-City as he was coming out of his office. The kidnappers demanded a very high ransom for his release. After days of difficult negotiations, the family consented to pay the ransom to the kidnappers and they waited several days before the man was finally released. He was found locked up in the trunk of a stolen car which had been parked in one of the busiest streets of the city. He had been banging on the lid for the last two or three hours before some passerby realized that the noise was coming from the trunk of the car. After this episode, the man hired three armed bodyguards to accompany him wherever he went.

We could not always depend on the protection offered by the police force because they were not reliable. Policemen received very low salaries and were eager to find ways of increasing their income by rendering favors to certain people. As a result, they often became accessories in various cases of corruption. In order to join the force, the Guatemalan authorities required that one purchase his uniform. Since most of those who were willing to enlist in the force did not have sufficient means to do so, they had to find sponsors in the community who would offer them their equipment and as a consequence, the newly drafted policemen felt they had a moral debt toward their benefactors.

When I went to the Customs office to find out how much I would have to pay in duties to import a used Chevrolet from the United States, they told me that it would amount to three thousand dollars. I said,

"In that case, I will give up the idea because the car is not worth this amount."

I was about to leave the office, when the clerk called me back and invited me to follow him in a little room. He then said:

"How much would you be willing to pay to import this car?"

"Three hundred dollars," I said, "might be reasonable."

"That is fine," said the officer, "just bring the money in cash to me personally and I will sign all the papers."

I refused to do this and I eventually bought a used car from one of the staff members of the American embassy who had completed his tour of duty.

After a year in the country, my family and I had to face a major crisis. Our son Dan, who was studying at the French School of Guatemala-City, got very sick one morning and went into a near-coma. He was taken to the emergency care section of a private clinic. We called the pediatrician recommended by the American embassy and he treated our son for what he thought was a case of a bad flu. When I realized that there was no improvement after two days, I called a neurologist who had been trained in France to examine our son. He almost immediately diagnosed our son's illness. He was suffering from meningitis. After administering the proper antibiotics, Dan was able to recover without any apparent side-effect.

My wife became quite fluent in Spanish before any of us because she would spend much time talking to the women working behind the stalls at the downtown Farmers Market. When she realized that most of them could not read or write, she took the initiative of organizing literacy classes for them at the market so that they might be able to read the official notices they were receiving and keep track of their sales.

When the representative of the Jewish Agency in Central America received instructions to organize a National Bible Contest in conjunction with the Israeli Committee supervising the selection of candidates, he invited me to participate in the project. We were to find the best Bible students in the country. We organized various quizzes in different cities and we invited the best candidates to compete among themselves. My task consisted of preparing the many questions which would enable us to proceed with our contest. I spent two months frantically re-reading the various books of the Hebrew Bible in order to formulate interesting questions which would be used during the quizzes.

The last two sessions were broadcast on live television and they became a sort of national event. The winner of the contest was a Mestizo of Mayan extraction who was a member of the *Iglesia de Dios* (Church of God), a Sabbath observing Protestant denomination in Latin America. The members of this group would spend practically every Saturday studying the Bible in their churches. Our national champion received a grant to fly to New York to participate in the next stage of the selecting process. The best candidates were eventually invited to Jerusalem to participate in the final Bible Quiz or *H'idon Ha-Tanakh* as they call it in Israel. It was a most rewarding project for me and I was pleased to see that it was greatly appreciated by the community at large and the members of my congregation.

When I learned that there were descendants of Jews living in Quetsaltenango, a middle-sized city nested high in the mountains, I suggested to my congregation that we spend a Sabbath week-end with them. That excursion proved to be one of the most exciting adventures I had during my stay in the country. On a Friday morning, a dozen congregants and I drove to the city. Upon our arrival, we met with the representatives of the group. They were the children and grandchildren of Lebanese

Jews who had settled there some fifty years before. They had all inter-married with Indian and Mestizo women and assimilated to the mores of the region. However, some of them still had nostalgic memories of their ancestral tradition.

We held Sabbath services in an old colonial house and there were tears in the eyes of the elders. We sang Sephardic songs in Hebrew and Ladino (ancient Castilian Spanish) which a few remembered from their parents and grandparents. We had a festive dinner together and we chatted for hours while their spouses and their children wondered why they were so moved by our celebration. These lovely people had lived in this remote mountain town of Central America like the *Marranos,* the Crypto-Jews of the Iberian peninsula. Their identification with the Jewish people had seemingly faded away when they decided to become an integral part of the local population.

Some time later, the National Federation of Temple Youth invited me and my youth group to participate in a regional gathering which took place in Mexico-City. It was a great opportunity for all of us to connect with other youth groups from the United States.

IV

THE MEXICAN INDIAN JEWS OF
VENTA-PRIETA

The members of the Guatemalan group were delighted to meet with their new friends from the southern region of the United States. When our Mexico-City conclave came to an end, Rabbi Samuel Cook, the national director of the National Federation of Temple Youth, his wife and I decided one afternoon to visit the community of *the Mexican Indian Jews* of Venta Prieta, some fifty miles north of the Mexican capital. We took a taxi and we drove toward the state of Hidalgo until we arrived in that little town of three hundred fifty inhabitants. We met with Señor Tellez, the president of the Jewish community, who took us to their little synagogue and explained to us that half of the inhabitants of their town were following the teachings of Judaism. He expressed the regret, however, that the Jews of Mexico-City did not recognize them as Jews.

"Why is it so?" asked Rabbi Cook.

"It is because we were not converted by a rabbinical authority," said Mr. Tellez.

"So, if you underwent a formal conversion," said rabbi Cook, "the Jewish community would regard you as bona fide Jews. I will see what I can do about it."

Rabbi Cook was very sensitive to the plea of Señor Tellez and when we left Venta Prieta to return to Mexico-City, he spoke to me in the taxi:

"Leo, since you know Spanish and are familiar with the Latin American scene, I would like to invite you to direct a summer project for our youth groups from the New York and Texas areas who would like to do some volunteer work in this community. The youngsters might be of service to these people in more than one way. You will have to design a program and be responsible for a group of some twenty to twenty five older teenagers and university students. We might call it the *Mexican Mitzvah Corps* and it will be like a Peace Corps program for Jewish youth."

"I think it will be a great challenge and a service to this community," I said, "I will discuss this matter with my wife and I will let you know in the next few days."

Susan and I agreed to assume this responsibility.

I returned to Venta Prieta a few weeks later and I scouted the area to find an inn or a hotel where our youngsters could stay for four weeks. In the absence of such a place in the town, I made an agreement with the owner of an old colonial hotel in near-by Pachuca, the capital of the state of Hidalgo. The hotel had been closed for a year for lack of customers. The owner was glad to rent the whole hotel to us for four weeks . I also found a restaurant-cantina near the hotel where we could have most of our meals. I hired the driver of an old bus to take us to Venta Prieta every day and bring us back in the late afternoon. The project I conceived would require that most of the volunteers work on the construction of a meeting-hall just next door to the synagogue. I wrote to Rabbi Cook in New York to let him know that I had completed my preparation. He then proceeded to inform the various youth groups about the project and the registrations soon began to come in.

Two months later, some twenty two volunteers arrived in Mexico-City from the United States. A minibus took them from the airport to our hotel in Pachuca. The next morning, Pedro came to fetch us and took us to Venta Prieta to meet with our friends as we had agreed in our correspondence but the leaders of the community were all gone. The president's wife and several of her friends showed us around the village as we waited for the men to arrive. They acknowledged that they had received my letter, but they did not believe that twenty two American students would be wiling to spend four weeks with them in their little town. They were happy to see us full of enthusiasm and willing to get acquainted with them. I asked for their full cooperation so that we may build a communal hall in the following four weeks and we finalized our plans together

In order to proceed, we needed to buy bricks and cement and hire two masons to assist us in the construction. Some of the young people in the congregation expressed the desire to join our group. We agreed to carry the bricks, mix the cement and assist the masons in the actual building of the walls. I bought all the material including some sheets of corrugated cement to serve as a roof, some ceiling windows and a large door made of wrought iron. We divided the work and every participant had a specific task to perform. Those who were not involved in the construction of the hall agreed to teach literacy classes or basic English to the villagers. We soon started our work with great excitement and it was a pleasure to see this group of middle-class university students work on the construction site.

During a break from our work, one of the elders of the congregation, Don Gregorio, took me aside one day and said:

"*Señor Rabino*, I would like to ask you a favor. I would like to learn how to conduct a service the way they lead services in the synagogues of Mexico-City. Can you teach me?"

I was very touched by the request and I said: "Certainly, Don Gregorio, I will give you a private lesson every other day and you will soon be able to conduct a service with some mastery."

We celebrated the Sabbath together with our new friends and we learned about the lives of the members of the community. They believed that they were the descendants of the *Marranos* (crypto-Jews), who came from Spain at the time of the *Conquista* and who had inter-married with Indian women. They told us amazing stories which often sounded like fairy tales. I later learned from a Mexico-City professor, that they first joined a Sabbath-observing church, *la Iglesia de Dios,* by the end of the nineteenth century. Several generations later, a part-time minister, Licenciado Laureano Balthazar Ramirez, led them to believe that they were all the descendants of the Jews who came from Spain, that is the Israelites mentioned in the Bible. They adopted the Star of David as their symbol and transformed their church into a synagogue. They were now hoping to be recognized as full-fledged members of the Jewish religion.

We completed our project in three and a half weeks. I then sent a letter to several Jewish organizations in Mexico-City to invite their members to the dedication of the social hall. I made sure to send also an invitation to the mayor and the Catholic bishop of Pachuca. Two days later, as I was on my way to our construction site to supervise the painting of the hall, I was arrested by the Mexican immigration police who took me to their main office in Mexico-City. I had been denounced for practicing the ministry in the country without a proper permit from the authorities. Indeed, Mexican law stipulates that no non-Mexican citizen has the right to preach religion in Mexico. This law was meant to protect the Roman Catholic Church from the activities of missionaries who were keen on getting converts away from the established church. I was in good company at the immigration office with a dozen young Mormons and several other missionaries who had been arrested on that same day on similar charges.

When the reporter of the *New York Times* called for an interview, my wife let him know that I had been apprehended by agents of the immigration department. The reporter then called the security officer of the American Embassy to inform him about my arrest. The officer then called the department and requested my release. In spite of his intervention, I spent most of the day in the custody of the immigration officers. When I was finally introduced to the deputy in charge, he said to me,

"Señor, we had no alternative but to arrest you because we received a report stating that you had sent an invitation to several officials which was signed by you as a rabbi."

"That is correct," I said, "but it was not for the purpose of converting Mexican citizens to Judaism. My volunteers and I came to Mexico to work on a joint project with the members of the Venta Prieta community. We have been busy building a hall at our own expense and we hope that it will enhance their community life."

" Señor," he then said, "we appreciate what you have done but I must warn you not to say anything during the dedication ceremony which might be construed as a message inviting people to convert to Judaism. I wish you good luck."

As I was leaving the Immigration office, I remembered that I had sent only two invitations to non-Jewish officials: the mayor and the bishop of the city of Pachuca.

I was wondering whether any of their secretaries had informed the authorities.

Over one hundred people from the area and the capital attended the dedication including Mr. Albert Vorspan, the vice-president of the Union of American Hebrew Congregations who flew from New York in order to attend the event. I asked my assistant, Jay Heyman, a Hebrew Union College rabbinical student, to conduct the ceremony. I said a few words to thank our guests and especially our volunteers from the United States and Venta Prieta who had so generously given of their time and effort to build this hall which would become a symbol of our mutual friendship. I affixed the Mezuzah (scroll containing two passages from Scriptures) to the doorpost at the entrance of the hall. As soon as we concluded the ceremony, two Mexican visitors whom I did not know, came to me and asked to be converted. I had been warned about this possible happening and I said,

"Friends, we came here to work on a joint project with the community of Venta Prieta and we built together this social hall, but we did not come here to convert anyone."

They were, without any doubt, trying to test me to see if I would break the agreement I had made with the immigration officer in Mexico-City. I never found out who had denounced me to the authority.

The next day, I received a call from the security officer of the American embassy who inquired about my well-being and who let me know that the Ambassador would be pleased to invite me and my family and all the volunteers in our group to attend a reception at the embassy in Mexico-City. In addition, the reporter of the New York Times let us know that he had written a three column article on our mission of good-will and that it would be published the next day. All the volunteers were happy to have participated in this project of Jewish solidarity.

I had completed my assignment in Mexico and I was ready to pursue my career in new surroundings. Since the World Union for Progressive Judaism still did not have an opening in France, its director suggested that I apply for the pulpit of the Spanish and Portuguese Congregation Mikve Israel-Emanuel on the island of Curaçao in the Netherlands Antilles. The congregation was affiliated with the Reconstructionist Federation of Congregations as well as the World Union. The newly formed congregation was the result of a recent merger between Congregation Mikve Israel and Temple Emanuel. The first was the oldest synagogue in the Americas which still followed the traditional Sephardic ritual. Temple Emanuel had seceded from the mother synagogue nearly a century before to join the Reform movement. My family and I agreed to pursue our career in Curaçao in order to comply with my original commitment.

V

THE OLDEST SYNAGOGUE IN THE AMERICAS

I arrived in the sunny island of Curaçao at the beginning of January 1967 for an interview with the directors of the congregation. I was asked to conduct Sabbath services, preach a couple of sermons and give a lecture on a Jewish theme in the conference room of a hotel. The synagogue, with its mahogany ceiling, its brass chandeliers and yellow sand on the floor, was packed to capacity with some three or four hundred worshippers seated in the pews and many standing all around the walls inside and behind the large open windows, all dressed in fine casual clothes. When I asked the president if all the participants were members of the congregation, he answered me casually: "Not all of them, Rabbi." I later learned that only about fifty or sixty people were actually members of the congregation and the other three hundred were tourists from the U.S. and Canada. I conducted the Friday and Saturday services which were accompanied by an organ and I delivered my sermons to the satisfaction of the members and the tourists. The congregation offered me a three year contract and I resolved to adopt the Spanish and Portuguese tradition of my new congregation.

My family and I made plans to travel to our new destination in the southern part of the Caribbean sea. Since clergy people are considered employees of the government in the Netherlands and the Dutch possessions, the authorities gave us the choice between flying to the island or traveling by ship. We chose to take a cruise-ship because the shipping company would allow us to take more luggage with us. We rented a house and registered our children at a near-by public school where they were taught in the Dutch language for it was the official language of the island. The local population, including most of the Jews, spoke *Papiamento*, a composite language made up of Spanish and Portuguese, some Dutch, French, English and even a few words of Hebrew. They also spoke Spanish and English with the many tourists who visited the island all year long. The synagogue services were conducted in Hebrew and English but the prayer for the welfare of the Queen and the royal family of the Netherlands was recited in Portuguese as it had been the tradition for the past three hundred fifty years.

The *Snoa* - short for *sinagoga* - was an impressive monument of great character. It was patterned after the Spanish and Portuguese synagogue of Amsterdam and had been built in the eighteenth century. After the Jews were expelled from Spain and Portugal in 1492, many of them sought refuge in the Netherlands. When the Dutch settled in Brazil at the beginning of the seventeenth century, several hundred *Sephardic* (Spanish) families joined them and established Jewish communities in the north-eastern part of the country. They prospered there for four decades until the Portuguese navy arrived in 1651 and gave the Dutch three months to leave the country. Many returned to Holland, but others settled in Surinam (Dutch Guiana) and six Caribbean islands which included Curaçao. The Dutch deported the small garrison of Spaniards and the Indians who were living on the island. A few hundred Dutch families settled on these new shores including a small number of Jews. In the years which followed, other descendants of the

Spanish and Portuguese Jews came to join this first group.

Though it was isolated geographically from the rest of the world, life was quite pleasant on the island. We were surrounded by the sea on all sides and one could go swimming in the blue Caribbean waters at any time of the year. We got accustomed to the high temperatures of the summer. As in many tropical areas, all the stores and offices were closed between twelve and four in the afternoon, to enable everyone to have a siesta during the warmest hours of the day.

Between January and the end of April, large numbers of tourists would visit the island and attend Friday night services. Those who intended to go to the casinos later in the evening, would often ask me if there was a special prayer for good luck they might recite. I would answer them facetiously:

"Yes, there is a passage in the Bible which refers to good and bad fortune. It is found in Psalm 91 and it explicitly says: *A thousand may fall at your left hand side and ten thousand at your right hand, but it shall not reach you.*' This verse," I would say to them, "aptly describes what will happen to you at the casino. You will come close to one thousand and even ten thousand, but you will probably not win anything. I would recommend that you read that psalm before you go down to the casino tonight. You may find it in the Gideon Bible that is in the drawer of your bedside table."

The members of the congregation were always intrigued by the crowd of visitors who attended services. They did not know that the directors of tourism aboard most of the cruise-ships making a stop-over in Curaçao, would strongly recommend that they visit the most ancient synagogue of the Americas which has been in continuous existence for three hundred years.

For sound economic reasons, the Department of Tourism commissioned an American Public Relations firm to find out the whereabouts of the tourists who were coming to the island so that they might make their visit more pleasurable. When the results of the survey were released, they showed that a large number of tourists were of the Jewish faith. The Commissioner of Tourism of the island invited me to become a consultant to his commission so that I might advise him on ways of attracting more tourists to the island. I took upon myself to double the number of guided tours of the synagogue every morning during the high season. I would tell my audience about the history of the community and the circumstances which had led it to affiliate with the Jewish Reconstructionist movement a few years before.

"What is Reconstructionism" they would ask, and I would be pleased to give them a mini-lecture on the various branches of the Jewish community. Others would ask:

"Who are the Sephardic Jews?" and I would give them a short talk on Jewish history.

We had a guest book at the entrance of the synagogue and many would sign it as they were leaving the synagogue. When we were about to welcome the ten thousandth visitor of the season, we arranged for a photographer to be present at that moment and we celebrated the event by offering a present to the lucky visitor. A middle-aged woman from Los Angeles almost cried when we announced that she would receive the prize in the presence of a crowd of visitors. She may not have won anything at the casino that evening, but she had received an ovation for visiting the synagogue.

On Thursday afternoon, I would conduct a half hour religious program on the local television station. I often interviewed some of the personalities who happened to visit the island. Many spectators had become familiar with my program and when they met me in the street, they would be pleased to greet me. On other days of the week, a Catholic priest and a Protestant minister would conduct their own religious programs.

There was another Jewish community on the island. It was the synagogue of the Eastern European Jews who had arrived as refugees before or during the war. Some had been interned in camps when they arrived in Curaçao during the war but they were later released when the authorities were reasonably convinced that they were not Nazi collaborators. The members of this congregation remained faithful to the Orthodox Eastern European tradition. Though a merger of the two congregations was not contemplated, an agreement was reached between them to establish a united religious school and a joint youth group for all the Jewish children. The leaders of the two groups thought that this rapprochement would constitute a first step toward better relations between the liberal and the traditional congregations. My Orthodox colleague and I were both involved in the religious school teaching.

A number of *intra-faith* marriages took place between the members of the two congregations. In the course of time, some of the *Ashkenazi* (Eastern European) Jews joined the Sephardic synagogue and some became members of the two congregations. When I announced an introduction to the Talmud class, I was quite surprised by the fact that several Dutch Christian attorneys and members of the Orthodox congregation signed up for the class. I also met many people of African background who confessed to me that they were descendants of Jews. They were usually proud of their Jewish ancestry. Unlike any other country I had known before, I did not experience the slightest manifestation of anti-semitism during the three years my family and I spent in Curaçao. I would even dare say that there was a strong philo-semitism on the island and that those who could not point to some Jewish ancestor, wished they had one.

A black man, who was the natural son of a prominent member of the congregation and a woman of African descent, asked me to teach him the principles of the Jewish faith. I gladly accepted to give him private lessons. When I realized that he was ready for a formal conversion, I requested permission from the board of directors to proceed with the ceremony. Ismael Francisca thus became the first Black man on the island to convert to Judaism.

Ismael was a tall and corpulent man who worked for the administration of the island. After he studied the basics of the Jewish religion and learned to read Hebrew, he memorized a passage of the Torah and he celebrated his Bar Mitzvah in the synagogue. From that day on he never missed a prayer service at the synagogue and he watched secretly over the synagogue to make sure that no one would dare desecrate it.

When a reporter-photographer from National Geographic came to Curaçao to prepare an article for his magazine, I accompanied him through the synagogue and answered all his questions to the best of my abilities. When he asked me whether there were black members of the congregation, I told him that we actually had one who had just converted to Judaism. He then asked me if he could take some pictures with him in the synagogue. He formally promised me that he would state in his article that this man was the first black man who had converted to Judaism on the island of Curaçao.

I called my friend Ismael and he came to the synagogue as soon as he was able to do so. The reporter began to take photographs of the synagogue and Ismael. The secretary of the synagogue who thought there was something unusual taking place in the synagogue, called a member of the board to let him know about the photographer. He immediately came to the synagogue and he told the reporter that he had no right to take these photographs without permission and that he should not publish those he had already taken. Ismael and I felt terribly embarrassed and so was the reporter who sent me one of the kindest letters I ever received, in order to apologize for the incident that had taken place that morning in the synagogue. The board member did not want the readers of the magazine to get the erroneous impression that the congregation was predominantly a black congregation.

In May 1969, just a few months after this incident, tension grew between the labor unions, essentially black workers, and the management of the Shell refinery, the largest employer on the island. In an attempt to reorganize its management, the refinery had decided to divest itself of the responsibility of certain categories of employees. The workers involved in the cleaning and maintenance of the plant were placed under the direction of a private company which offered to rehire them but at a lower salary than they were getting before. The labor unions felt that their members had a legitimate grievance and they insisted that the workers receive a salary equal to the one they had previously received. As the managers of the new company refused to negotiate these matters, the labor unions, inspired by the ideology of the Black Power movement, decided to organize a general strike on the island.

On the appointed day, the strikers started to march through the main streets of Willemstad carrying signs and banners, but the march soon degenerated into a series of riots and acts of violence. Some radical elements had taken advantage of the strike to create havoc on the island by setting commercial buildings afire. As the situation got out of hand, the local government decided to call in the military forces stationed on the island to help them restore order, but the only individuals who had authority to call the army, i.e. the governor and vice governor of the Netherlands Antilles, were out of the country and inaccessible by telephone. Given these circumstances, the order had to be issued by the Dutch government. This process took several hours.

During that time, a number of businesses and private houses in Willemstad were engulfed in flames. As a result of the rioting, several people were killed and some hundred fifty people had to be hospitalized. Many residents had hastily fled the island in their private airplanes or in rented planes which were sent from neighboring Venezuela. The army finally intervened in the late afternoon and re-established order on the island but the provincial government of the Netherlands Antilles eventually collapsed.

When the rioting began in the downtown area, my wife happened to be in the leading jewelry store where she was working on a part-time basis. She was able to leave the store in great haste to go home and take care of our children. As for me, I was in my office at the synagogue and Ismael came by to make sure everything was fine. He suggested that we close the synagogue and he offered to accompany me to my car so that I might go home and join my family. In order to reach the lot where my car was parked, we had to pass a roadblock. Ismael only said a few words in Papiamento and we were allowed to pass. We then took a shortcut which required that we cross a ditch. He spontaneously took me in his arms and deposited me on the other side. He wished me good luck and said,

"I must return to Punda and I want to make sure that nothing happens to our Snoa."

I felt that Ismael had protected me just as the Ethiopian mercenary Eved Melech had saved prophet Jeremiah, as we find narrated in the biblical account.

Due to the unwillingness of the labor unions to talk to the remaining officials on the island, it became necessary to find some trustworthy notables to serve as intermediaries between them. The members of the clergy were thus called in to serve in that capacity. The Catholic bishop, the chairman of the Council of Churches and I, as the representative of the Jewish community, got involved in the delicate task of helping the parties reach an understanding and find a solution to the conflict that was opposing labor and management. My colleagues and I spent six entire days and portions of the night listening to the labor union representatives and offering many suggestions until we eventually succeeded in convincing them to give up the violent confrontation and simply demand new elections. We assured them that once elected to the parliament of the Netherlands Antilles, they would be able to play an important role in the next government and be instrumental in bringing about the social and political changes they were seeking. It devolved on me to explain to the Longshoremen's Union leader how democratic elections function. I assured him that he and several of his colleagues would, no doubt, be elected to the next parliament and that he would surely become a member of the cabinet and possibly the minister of labor. He then asked me:

"Will I then ride in a black limousine and will a driver take me around?"

When I assured him that this would most likely be the case, he felt quite satisfied and said,

"Then, let's have elections!"

I delivered a passionate appeal for calm and peace in Papiamento in my weekly television program. Ron Gomes Casseres, the son of my congregation's president helped me translate my address and rehearse it until I pronounced it almost correctly. A month later, new elections took place and I was fortunate to see my prediction come true. The president of the Longshoremen union was elected and eventually made a member of the cabinet. That was my first experience as a peace maker in a labor dispute that could have caused more violence and destruction than it did. Calm and tranquility returned on the island and new programs of social and cultural development were implemented.

This confrontation had resulted from an error on the part of the management of the Wescar company that had taken over the responsibility for the maintenance of the Shell Refinery. Except for that incident, there existed a friendly relationship between the various ethnic segments of the population and the religious communities on the island. As a consequence, I took part in a number of unusual ecumenical and cultural activities during the three years of my tenure on the island. I became a member of the Inter-faith committee which had undertaken to translate the Bible in Papiamento. We began our project by working on the translation of a small book of the Bible, the book of Jonah. My task consisted of sharing with my colleagues the exact meaning of the Hebrew original text. I also became involved in the creation of an academy of the Papiamento language, which I thought would be a good way of recognizing the cultural and linguistic identity of the indigenous population of the island.

One morning, the secretary of the congregation knocked at the door of my office and whispered to me that the Imam of the Islamic community wanted to speak to me. I welcomed him with the proper *Salaam Aleikum* and invited him to take a seat. He was dressed in his traditional robe and he explained to me that he had just arrived from Egypt. He spoke little English but we were able to communicate quite well. He had come to see me for a specific reason. He had just received a book on Egyptian history which contained a few pages that had left him deeply confused and perplexed. Indeed, the author of the book was stating that the Hebrews had never been slaves in Egypt and that this whole story had been invented by the Jews to shed a dark picture on the Egyptians.

"But that cannot be" said the Imam, "because the holy Koran mentions these facts explicitly and the Hebrew Bible too, if I am correct."

I fully agreed with him and we came to the conclusion that the author of the book was simply disregarding the account found in our respective Holy Scriptures and was only intent in pursuing a polemical argument against the Jews.

There was a small Muslim community on the island formed mainly of immigrants from Lebanon and Syria. They had settled on the island when they realized it was an ideal place where they could practice international trade with the Latin American continent and sell goods to the many tourists visiting the island. Indeed, hundreds of buyers and quite a few smugglers from Venezuela and

Colombia were coming to Curaçao every day to do their shopping in the free port of Willemstad.

On special occasions, I accompanied my wife and my children in order to perform some charitable tasks on behalf of the Curaçao Association of American Women. On Christmas day, my whole family would visit several homes for the aged and organize a little pageant during which we distributed presents to the residents on behalf of the association. My children derived a great deal of pleasure from singing "We wish you a merry Christmas…" and other carols they had learned at school, knowing full well that they were only singing these songs to cheer up the elderly folks and that they did not express their personal convictions. These homes were quite primitive in terms of American standards. My children were shocked by the fact that many of the elderly folks were lying on mattresses made of straw on boxes made of plain wood. A strong odor filled the dormitories. The residents were very appreciative for the kindness we were showing them. Those who had seen me on television were particularly grateful to see *el pastor*, because for them any man of the cloth was a pastor and it did not matter whether he belonged to one religion or another.

On one occasion, I helped organize a concert by the Los Angeles Jewish Doctors Symphony, a group of physicians who were also accomplished musicians. We had a full house at the synagogue that evening. Jews and non-Jews alike, were delighted to hear such a fine orchestra perform on the island. The doctors thanked us for the privilege which had been granted them to perform in the oldest synagogue in the Americas and they even made substantial donations to the synagogue and the rabbi's discretionary fund which I immediately channelled to the Reconstructionist Foundation.

On another occasion, I had the honor of escorting Andre Chouraqui, who spent a whole week in Curaçao on a business and leisure trip. He was the secretary general of the *Alliance Israelite Universelle,* the French agency which had established an extended network of French Jewish schools in various Mediterranean countries, I also gave several lectures to the members of the *Alliance Française*, the French cultural society, which included a number of Dutch people who had a good knowledge of the French language and a keen interest in French culture.

When the old house adjacent to the social hall of the synagogue was restored, I was called by the foreman of the crew one morning, and he showed me that they had found an oval construction just two feet under the ground in front of the building. I immediately identified the *Mikvah*, the ritual bath, that must have been part of the Snoa compound. It was located right under the roof of that house so that it might collect the rain water during the short rainy season. It was built with the same yellow bricks which were used in the construction of many old buildings on the island, and which had been brought from Holland as ballast on freight ships in centuries past. This ancient house which may have served as the residence of the rabbi at one time - and the Mikvah – was eventually remodeled to house the Jewish Museum of the island.

As we were about to conclude our third year on the island, my wife and I were happy to welcome the birth of our third child and second daughter. Linda Michelle was born on a Friday night at the exact time the members of the synagogue were welcoming the Sabbath. Indeed, the moment her mother felt that the time had come, I let the president know that I would not go to synagogue that evening, and instead, my wife and I went straight to the Maternity. As we were waiting to be admitted, I recited the Shabbat eve psalms as I would have done at the synagogue and when I arrived to the hymn *Lekha Dodi* (come, my beloved) her mother indicated that she could no longer wait. She was immediately led into the delivery room where our daughter was born at the exact moment the faithful were reciting the concluding words of the hymn: *Boi khalah, boi khala, Welcome Bride, Welcome Bride!*

After these three years on the island, my family and I felt we had become nearly authentic Sephardic Jews. I had learned to recite some prayers in ancient Portuguese from the pulpit and chant the Haphtarah according to the traditional Sephardic melody. I began to study the history of the Jews of Spain and Portugal and later wrote a few essays on the subject. One of them was posted on the Internet for several years. As we were about to leave the island for the United States, the board of directors invited Robert Silverman, a rabbinical student who was studying at the Leo Baeck Rabbinical College in London, to insure the transition between my departure and the coming of my successor. Robert was an enthusiastic young man with red hear who was extremely conscientious and eager to learn the customs and ceremonies of the Spanish and Portuguese rite. He later returned to London and became a rabbi in Manchester.

A few days before our departure from Curaçao, the congregation organized a lovely farewell party in the Sala, the social hall of the synagogue, and we said goodbye to all our friends. I had now completed five years of service to the World Union for Progressive Judaism instead of the three which were part of my contractual obligation. My wife and I were looking forward to settling in the United States where our children would be able to learn English at school.

VI

BACK TO THE UNITED STATES

My wife and my children flew to San Francisco to spend a few weeks with the family while I remained in New York in order to meet with the director of placement of my rabbinical association. After five years of isolation away from a Jewish cultural center, I was eager to find a post in a large metropolis like New York and with a congregation that was tradition-minded. I was advised to apply for the pulpit of a small Reform congregation in Pearl River, a short drive from New York. I arranged to meet with their rabbi's search committee and at the appointed time, I arrived at the building which served as a place of worship. We all sat down around a large board table. The committee chairman opened the meeting with a few words of welcome and then he addressed me and said:

"Rabbi, before we discuss congregational matters, I would like to ask you a personal question: 'What do you think of the Vietnam war'?"

I was quite surprised by the question and I simply answered,

"Ladies and gentlemen, I have been away from the United States for the last five years and as a consequence, I only have a scant understanding of the issue at stake and have not been able to form a clear opinion about it."

The committee chairman seemed to be satisfied with my answer and he said,

"Now we can proceed with our interview."

I later learned that he was an active member of the American Legion and that the previous rabbi of the congregation had taken a strong stand against the Vietnam war which greatly displeased the chairman. Consequently, the rabbi's contract had not been renewed and he was also looking for a new position. It was a classical Reform congregation and it soon became clear that we had different expectations in terms of religious life.

When I explained to the placement director that I was looking for a more traditional congregation, he arranged an interview for me with the search committee of a modern Orthodox Sephardic congregation in Los Angeles, whose president was a friend of his. I flew to Los Angeles and after spending a week-end with the congregation and meeting with the committee, I gathered the impression that the members were all very attached to the tradition of the Jewish community of Rhodes from which they originated. They had only made one concession to the American way of life: they had decided to allow men and women to sit together in their synagogue. I told the president of the congregation that I did not think I was the right candidate for the post and I returned to New York.

While in the city, I established a friendly relation with Rabbi Arthur Gilbert, who was involved in the development of the Reconstructionist movement and the creation of a new Rabbinical College in Philadelphia. As he was also serving as the interim director of placement for the movement, he offered to help me find a position with one of the congregations which had contacted his office in order to find a rabbi. Within a few days, he arranged two interviews with New Jersey Conservative congregations.

These congregations had turned to the Reconstructionist movement to find a rabbi because they were particularly concerned about an impending resolution of the United Synagogue of America to suspend all congregations organizing bingo games on their premises. When I had my interview with the rabbi's selection committee of the first congregation, I was not asked about my stand on the war in Vietnam this time, but the chairman opened the meeting with these words:

"Rabbi, before we proceed with our interview, we would like to ask you if you would be offended by the fact that our congregation organizes bingo games in the social hall of our temple in order to raise funds for the general treasury. You must realize, Rabbi, that without this kind of additional income, we would be unable to pay your salary."

And then, with a big smile on his face, the chairman of the first congregation added:

"The games we organize are not meant for our members but for the residents who live in our area. In fact, we are providing a social service to the community at large."

I answered that I had no objection to holding bingo games as a fundraiser for the congregation. I said I was more interested in finding out if young couples were attending services with some regularity. The chairman of the congregation promptly replied: "You know, Rabbi, young people don't have much free time these days. They come for the High Holidays and on special occasions, but you cannot expect them to come every Saturday of the year. Retired people constitute the core of our participants at most of our services."

I did not pursue this avenue and I had another interview with the second congregation. With few variations, it began and finished on the same notes. They let me know that I expected too much from them and we agreed that I was not the kind of rabbi they were looking for. At the recommendation of Rabbi Gilbert, my search for a rabbinical post took me next to Birmingham, Alabama.

It was a large Conservative congregation whose vice-president was a great admirer of Prof. Mordecai Kaplan, the founder of the Reconstructionist movement. I was invited to conduct Shabbat services and preach on Friday night and Saturday morning and I became one of the two top candidates selected by the rabbi's search committee. I was invited a second time to allow the members of the congregation to make their final choice. I gave an excellent sermon on the meaning of the Kaddish prayer. At the end of the service, as I read the names of the members of the congregation whose Yarhrzeit (anniversary of the death) occurred that week, I included the names of the students that had been killed the day before by the National Guards at Kent State University during a demonstration against the mandatory draft and the Vietnam war. The vice-president who had been very friendly towards me, immediately changed his attitude toward me and he asked the committee to set aside my candidacy. I heard him say after the service that the National Guards had done the right thing and he added:

"The rabbi should not have added the names of the students killed during the shooting that took place when the situation got out of hand on the campus."

After these frustrating experiences, I decided to take a pause and I flew to San Francisco to join my family at my wife's parents' house.

VII

A CONGREGATION IN SILICON VALLEY

Ever since I left Geneva, I had not enjoyed walking through the avenues of a large city as much as I did in San Francisco. In Guatemala and Curaçao, many of the streets had no sidewalk and we had to be extremely careful not to stumble on some rock or fall in a hole on the side of the road. I felt as if I was in the Paris of California. I was almost envious of the mail carrier who spent hours walking in these streets to deliver letters into mail boxes. If my main concern had not been my urgent need to find a job in order to support my family, I would have strolled in these streets for hours too.

Since the placement bureau of the Central Conference of American Rabbis was unable to help me find a suitable position, I considered abandoning the rabbinate altogether. A career in teaching or counseling might have spared me from getting involved in the meanders of congregational politics. As I was about to make that decision, I saw an ad in the Jewish Bulletin which stated that a small congregation near San Jose was looking for a full-time rabbi. I got in touch with the president of the congregation who invited me to meet with the rabbi's search committee. They did not ask me what I thought of the Vietnam war or the propriety of organizing bingo games in the synagogue premises. They only asked me if I could conduct meaningful services, supervise the religious school and teach a few adult education classes. After inviting me to spend a Shabbat with the congregation, they offered me the post and I became the first full-time rabbi of Congregation David of Cupertino.

We held our services in the garage which was attached to a private house. The interior was used as a religious school and the corridor as an office. The congregation was affiliated with the United Synagogue of Conservative Judaism. We did not waste any time. My wife and I rented a house in near-by Saratoga and we moved to that lovely area which was to become known as Silicon Valley. Our place of worship was always full to capacity on Friday night. From the time of its inception, the congregation had held only Friday night services and the members had become accustomed to this practice which enabled them to play golf at leisure on weekends. As we seldom had a Saturday morning service, I asked the president of the congregation if we could do something about it,

"Rabbi," said the president, "it's your responsibility. If you can motivate some of us to come on Saturday mornings, we shall gladly do so."

It was all a matter of gentle persuasion and encouragement. I took upon myself to call the members in order to invite them to participate in our celebration. I scheduled my Bar/Bat Mitzvah lessons just before the Saturday service so that my students and their parents might stay for the service. With some perseverance, I succeeded in getting a quorum and even a relatively good attendance. The members of the congregation were willing to be reminded of their religious obligations and they often thanked me for doing so. I endeavored to challenge them and awaken their interest in various aspects of the Jewish religion that they had never learned or never properly understood.

Rather than follow the traditional approach of expounding the meaning of some passage of the Torah portion of the week, I focussed my attention on major themes of Jewish philosophy in my Friday night sermons, except on the third Friday of the month at which time we had a special program called "Ask the Rabbi." During that inter-active session, any of the participants could ask any question they had and I would do my best to answer them. This dialogue from the pulpit soon became a popular program and many members of the congregation would invite their friends to come along with them on these nights. In just a few months, our membership doubled in size, going from sixty to hundred twenty families. As our "place of worship" could no longer accommodate all the worshippers who were attending our services, we made arrangements to rent a hall at the near-by YMCA and a committee was formed to look into the possibility of acquiring a piece of land so that we might build a synagogue for the congregation.

The majority of the members of Temple David were engineers working for the Lockheed corporation and professionals who were practicing in the San Jose area. Most of them had a deep sense of commitment to Judaism and wanted their children to receive a good Jewish education. They were open to new ideas and new programs. The fact that I was a Hebrew Union College graduate did not matter to them. Since it was the only congregation in the area, it brought together Jews with different religious backgrounds. Some had belonged to Orthodox communities, others to Conservative or Reform temples before they came to California. The founders of the congregation had therefore agreed to settle for a compromise and had affiliated with the Conservative movement.

I had thus crossed the denominational boundaries which existed within the American Jewish community. I was a member of two national organizations, the Central Conference of American Rabbis and the Reconstructionist Foundation but I was at the service of a congregation affiliated with the United Synagogue of Conservative Judaism.

I had a verbal agreement with the congregation but no contract. Rabbi Arthur Gilbert of the Reconstructionist Foundation in New York was aware of this fact and he suggested that I consider moving ahead in my professional career. Upon his recommendation, I was contacted by the rabbi's search committees of two large congregations which were anxious to engage a Reconstructionist rabbi, one in Chicago and the other in Berkeley. Within a few weeks, Professor Philip Siegelman, a member of the board of directors of Temple Beth El in Berkeley came to see me one afternoon as he was on his way to San Jose State University. We had a friendly conversation and I was consequently invited for an interview by the rabbi's search committee of the congregation.

The search committee had already interviewed half a dozen candidates who had been recommended by the Central Conference of American Rabbis and as none of them had met with the expectations of the committee, the congregation had turned to the Reconstructionist Foundation in order to secure a suitable rabbi. The interview lasted three and a half hours until eleven thirty at night. The members of the search committee were particularly interested in finding out about my religious convictions and my belief in God, because they had read some critical essays on the Reconstructionist philosophy of religion. After that extended interview, they invited me to conduct Shabbat services on the following weekend and they offered me a five year contract. My family and I left Cupertino with some regret but I was looking forward to starting my career in a well established congregation in the Bay area.

VIII

IN THE WORLD OF ACADEMIA

We bought a house in the Berkeley Hills with a view of the San Francisco Bay. We registered our two older children at a near-by primary school and we hired a middle-aged African-American lady to take care of our youngest daughter during parts of the day. My wife was thus able to resume her studies at St Mary's College in Oakland in order to complete her bachelor's degree which had been put on hold on account of our traveling.

I developed a fine collegial relationship with Rabbi George Vida who had served as the interim rabbi while the congregation was looking for a permanent rabbi to fill the pulpit. He was a retired army chaplain originally from Hungary, who had come to live in Berkeley to be near his daughter and her family. We decided to work together in order to create a meaningful Shabbat morning service, which had not been part of the practice of Temple Beth El until then. I invited my colleague to participate in a Torah study which was held an hour before the service. It did not take long before we attracted over thirty people to these sessions. Most of them would stay for the service but some would leave after we had completed our study session because their desire to learn was greater than their desire to pray. In an expression of gratitude for his devoted service to the congregation, the board of directors later named Rabbi Vida, *scholar in residence* of Temple Beth El.

I conducted services with a part-time cantor and an organist who played an electric organ. In order to make the Friday evening service a celebration, I hired a musician and a folk dancing instructor who would animate the Oneg Shabbat after services. We were thus able to attract many young people who would never have come to synagogue if it had not been for this program. I invited members of the congregation to participate in the services by giving short sermons from time to time. I was agreeably surprised when the congregation accepted my suggestion to adopt a new Sabbath Prayerbook in order to replace the old Union Prayer Book which had become obsolete. We opted to acquire the prayer-book used by Reform congregations in Great Britain. After some research, we adopted the new High Holiday *Mah'zor* which had just been published by the United Synagogue of Conservative Judaism. The original features of this prayer-book resided in the fact that it contained many inspiring texts and meditations which had never been included in a prayer-book before.

I had been in my post for five or six weeks when I received a long letter from the executive vice-president of the Central Conference of American Rabbis to inform me, in no uncertain terms, that I should never have accepted the Berkeley post and to let me know that I had been suspended from my membership in the conference. No concern was expressed for the fact that they had been unable to help me find a position after five years of service abroad: two years in an extremely dangerous place and three years on an island far away from any academic institution of learning. They were reproaching me of having disregarded the rules of the Conference which required that a rabbi obtain permission to apply for any post with a Reform congregation.

They ignored the fact that I had a double allegiance and was a member of the Reconstructionist Foundation as well as the Conference. The leaders of the conference took advantage of this fact when they advised me to apply for the pulpit of the Curaçao congregation which was affiliated with two the religious organizations. They felt that this should not be permitted, however, in the United States. The executive vice-president of the conference asked the directors of Temple Beth El to rescind my contract but they refused to do so. They were informed that as a member of the Union of American Hebrew Congregations, they had broken a rule by inviting me to become their rabbi without their authorization. I was also informed that I would never be able to apply for a position with a congregation affiliated with the union of Reform congregations. I was condemned by my colleagues without any due process. I came to the conclusion that the leaders of the Reform movement were just as rigid and sectarian in their approach as their Orthodox counterpart.

My duties at Temple Beth El included the supervision of the religious school which was attended by some hundred sixty children. It emphasized the Sunday School curriculum rather than the Hebrew School one, which meant that very few students were learning Hebrew. As a consequence, we had a Confirmation ceremony each June but only two or three students were celebrating their Bar or Bat Mitzvah every year. I took upon myself to change this situation by organizing an intensive Hebrew class for twelve and thirteen year old students and their parents. Over twenty five students signed up for the class which lasted a whole year. We were then able to schedule Bar and Bat Mitzvah ceremonies which were all held during the Saturday morning service and not during the Friday night service as had been done previously.

From the day I assumed my post, various individuals, whether members of the congregation or not, would make appointments to see me in order to seek advice on personal and family matters which were not always related to Judaism. It gave me a great deal of satisfaction to be able to get involved in counseling. I came to realize, however, that my studies in child psychology and psychoanalysis were not sufficient to allow me to handle some of the intricate problems which were brought to my attention. In order to remedy this situation, I decided to acquire additional training in pastoral counseling and family therapy. I signed up for various seminars and summer courses at the extension of the University of California and San Francisco State

University and I also met with a clinical supervisor on a regular basis.

One morning, as I was walking on Shattuck Avenue in Berkeley, I met Dr Joseph Fabry, the founder of the Institute of Logotherapy and a friend of Viktor Frankl, whom I had met a few weeks before at a Bat Mitzvah reception. After a brief conversation, he invited me to register for an introductory course in logotherapy which was scheduled to begin the following week. I immediately accepted the invitation which could not have come at a better time since I had decided to develop my counseling skills. Joseph Fabry (formerly Epstein) was a quiet man who was passionate about the writings of Viktor Frankl. He was a native of Vienna, Austria and had just received a doctorate in law from the University when the *Anschluss* agreement between the Nazi regime and Austria was signed. As the Nazis began to apply the *Nuremberg laws* which forbade him to practice law in his country, he decided to immigrate to the United States and after a few years, he and his wife Judith settled in El Cerrito, California. He worked as an editor for the University of California Press until his retirement. He then devoted all his efforts to spreading the teachings of logotherapy in the United

States. He founded a magazine, the *International Forum for Logotherapy* which was published three times a year and he later organized an International Congress of Logotherapy which was held every other year in another city. The keynote address was always delivered by Prof. Viktor Frankl himself. I graduated from the Institute and made use of my newly acquired knowledge in counseling.

Together with a member of my congregation who was completing her doctoral thesis, I attended seminars at the San Francisco Jungian Institute. I also pursued Kabbalah studies at the Graduate Theological Union, an umbrella institution for post-graduate theological studies which included a section of advanced Judaic studies. I began teaching various adult education classes at the congregation and at the *Lehrhaus Judaica,* the Institute of Jewish studies of the Hillel Foundation, which was also open to members of the community. My classes were well attended and I was thus encouraged to pursue academic studies.

One evening, as I was teaching a class in Jewish mysticism and Kabbalah to some fifty adult students gathered in the social hall of the synagogue, I had an amazing experience. An elderly gentleman with white hair and a white beard came in and sat in the last row of the hall. He was very attentive to everything I was saying and at one time, he raised his hand and asked permission to speak. He stood up, came near the blackboard where I had written a few technical terms and he addressed the class with these words:

"I am delighted to see that you are studying the teachings of Kabbalah and I wish to congratulate you and your teacher. You see, I have been immersed in Kabbalah studies for the past sixty years ever since I was initiated by the late Chief Rabbi Abraham Cook of Palestine. I am pleased to let you know that I have found treasures of wisdom in these teachings. I hope that you too will find the way to true knowledge and faith in this pursuit."

The gentleman was Meyer Goldberg, a successful real-estate investor who was in his late eighties and who devoted most of his time and money to philanthropy and supporting Jewish institutions of learning in the United States and Israel. In the course of time, he became one of my spiritual mentors.

There were always unexpected visits at the Temple. One morning, a man who did not have an appointment knocked at the door of my office and said:

"Rabbi, I wish to salute you. I am Michael Lerner, do you know who I am?"

I invited him to take a seat and I said apologetically,

"I am new in the area. I have spent the last five years in the Caribbean and only one year in Saratoga near San Jose, and I do not know as yet everything I should know about the Bay area."

He then explained to me that he had worked with Mario Savio, the leader of the Free Speech Movement during its confrontation with the campus administration and the Berkeley police. He had come to invite me to the B'rith Milah (circumcision) of his son and to borrow my Rabbi's Manual so that he might officiate at the ceremony. I learned later that he had studied at the Jewish Theological Seminary for a few years before he decided to get a doctorate in political sciences. He taught at several universities and wrote several books and essays and was now the editor of *Tikkun* magazine. He had never abandoned the idea, however, of pursuing religious studies one day. He fulfilled his wish a number of years later when he was ordained as a rabbi by Reb Zalman Schachter, the charismatic founder of the Renewal Movement.

On another occasion, a young man came to see me to ask for advice on how to get along with his parents who had strongly objected to his having dropped out of his university studies. He reported to me that in his last conversation with his parents, he had said to them: "I just need a break in order to find myself." We discussed the matter freely, making sure that I would not impute guilt to any one. He thanked me profusely for having listened to him and as he was about to leave, he handed over to me a little bag that he took out of his pocket and said,

"Rabbi, this is good quality *grass* from Mexico."

Since I did not intend to smoke marijuana and was concerned about the fact that it was considered an illegal drug, I went to the bathroom and I flushed the little bag down the toilet. When I later related this peculiar incident to some of my new acquaintances, they expressed stupefaction at my attitude toward marijuana and one of them even said: "You did what…"

Berkeley had become the center of a cultural and political revolution. Some Maoists had taken over Freedom Park and various anti-war and anti-draft movements were organizing protests all over the city and the Bay area. When the president of the United

States, Richard Nixon, decided to bomb Cambodia, I saw thousands of young people protest in the streets of Berkeley. Some of them used violence and went on a rampage all over the main streets surrounding the University campus. They destroyed the windows of many stores and offices. The owner of a bookstore, whose windows had been shattered, placed a big sign on the door of his store the next day with the words, "Why did you break the windows of my store? I am your friend."

At the same time as this student revolution was taking place, religious sects were recruiting followers. Some of them had established residences for their new adepts so that they might keep them under their watch and make sure that they would not be tempted to leave the group. The new *gurus* would forbid their followers to communicate with their parents or friends except with their explicit permission. As a result, many parents were extremely distraught and wondering what had happened to their children. They would call the Berkeley police in the hope of getting some help to locate their children but the police would inform them that they were not sufficiently staffed to undertake such a demanding task. The next alternative available to parents was either to hire a private detective or call a compassionate clergyman who would be willing to assist them in their search.

As a consequence, I would often receive telephone calls from worried parents asking me to help them find out what had happened to their children. They would often mention the fact that the last time they had spoken to them, they were still studying at the university. Some had indicated that they were also studying with an Indian or an American-born guru or were about to move into one of the many communes which were mushrooming in Berkeley at the time. Several months had elapsed since that last call and they had not heard from their children. The new cult leaders often demanded full obedience from them. They would forbid their followers from having any contact with people who did not belong to the group.

When the parents of a young lady called me from Alabama, they told me that the last time they had spoken to her on the telephone, their daughter was about to move into the Ashram of Baba Muktenanda in Oakland. I called the residence several times and I left messages and I finally received an answer one morning. The young lady was willing to see me on condition that the Baba give his permission. I was told that I should first attend a prayer and meditation service and listen to a lecture-sermon one late afternoon and at the end of this gathering, I was allowed to see the Baba in a private room. He spoke through an interpreter though he knew English perfectly. When I told him that we did not need an interpreter, he answered me that it was the custom to do so. I told him that the parents of his new disciple were concerned about the well-being of their daughter and it was out of a sense of compassion for them that I was requesting permission to talk to her. We had a cordial exchange of ideas which lasted ten or fifteen minutes and then he said to me that the young lady was waiting to see me in the next room. The Baba blessed me and gave me a present and he anointed my forehead with musk. I thanked him for his kind gesture and he let me talk to the young lady.

She briefly told me her story and the reason she had not communicated with her parents. They had arranged a marriage for her and when she realized that it was not working out and she sought a divorce, her parents blamed her for her unwillingness to make compromises. She had then left her hometown and settled in San Francisco. A few months later, she entered the Ashram and stopped writing to her parents. She was glad to know, however, that her parents were concerned about her and she asked me to let them know that she was more happy now than she had been in Alabama. I told the parents that if they wanted to be reconciled with their daughter, they would have to apologize for their past behavior toward her for she had legitimate grounds for distancing herself from them.

On another occasion, I was asked to make contact with a follower of Reverend Sun Myung Moon, the former Korean Presbyterian Sunday School teacher, who declared himself to be a re-incarnation of God. The Church of the Reunification he had founded was attracting many followers in the Bay area and all over the country. I had to use a stratagem to enter the residence and locate the room of the lady I was looking for. She also had a personal reason for not corresponding with her parents. The cult leaders were exploiting those estrangements within the family to gain followers.

Master Rinpoche was teaching at the Tibetan Nyingma Institute in Berkeley for a few months every year and he too was attracting disciples. A Jewish young man from France came to see me one day and told me that he had registered for a complete course with the master and paid a handsome sum of money for this privilege. When he arrived in Berkeley, however, he was told that the spiritual master was teaching in India and that he should study with another teacher. While so many young people were under the hallowed influence of their new spiritual mentors, they would often forget all about their university studies and their families. On occasion, a disappointed disciple would break away from one of these groups and would come to ask me for moral support and guidance. I would thus get a first hand report on what was happening in these communal homes.

The Vietnam war had produced a social and cultural upheaval in the nation which affected especially those who might be drafted into the army. They were desperately seeking ways of overcoming the existential anxiety they were experiencing. In the meantime, clever charlatans were trying to assert their power over the minds of these distraught young people. Taking advantage of the confusion and distress that was widespread, they offered cultic panaceas to the spiritually starving young Americans. Jack Rosenberg, better known by the alias Werner Erhard, proposed a new approach to life in his Erhard Seminars Training or EST. A large segment of the members of my congregation registered for his first seminar. They came to believe that EST was the true path to happiness until they discovered that Werner Erhard was a charlatan and that his training was not worth the money they had invested in it.

The most difficult problem I had to face was related to the religious school. The teachers who had been hired before I came to the congregation simply refused to follow the curriculum and were each teaching whatever they wanted. One teacher, who had spent a year in Israel, thought that the children should learn about the way of life in the *Kibbutz* (Israeli collective farm). He transformed his classroom into a model farm with buckets of earth and plants all over the floor. The school committee did not have the will to fire that teacher because they had hired him in the first place. The mood of rebellion was in the air and it was not easy to overcome it. I had to wait till the end of the school year to ask the school committee to hire a part-time principal to deal with the school and its teachers.

On October 6, 1973, I routinely listened to the news in my car on my way to the synagogue to conduct the Yom Kippur services. I was distressed to learn that the armies of five Arab states had attacked Israel and were advancing on all fronts. Another war was being waged on Israel only six years after the Six Day war. Before I began the service, I informed the congregation that another war was being waged against Israel. Our Israeli brethren had to leave their synagogue in great haste to join their military units and be ready for combat. I offered a prayer for peace and solidarity and I asked the members of my congregation to pray with additional fervor, not only for themselves but for their Israeli brethren who would not be able to do so on this day. We then proceeded with our service for the Day of Atonement in a mood of profound sadness.

The following day, I called a dozen Christian colleagues from the Berkeley Ecumenical Council and I invited them to sign a simple statement expressing our hope that a peaceful resolution to the crisis would soon be found, but they all refused to do so, one after the other.

"There is another side to the story, you know…" a Baptist minister said to me.

"I will not support Israel this time…" said a Lutheran minister. I answered:

"It has nothing to do with supporting one country or another. It is peace in the region that we wish to pray for."

They were willing to protest the war in Vietnam but not the war which was being waged by five Arab nations determined to destroy the little state of Israel.

After making a dozen more telephone calls, I gave up my attempt to have a motion endorsed by the Berkeley clergy and I was extremely disappointed. For the last few years, I had supported my colleagues on various social and ethical issues. I had accompanied them to City Hall on a number of occasions and participated in various protests but when I needed their help and was asking them to sign a brief statement expressing our hope for peace in the Middle East, they all had a reason for refusing to do so. Fortunately, upon the advice of Secretary of State, Henry Kissinger, the president of the United States, Richard Nixon, promptly intervened to help the Israeli army regain its position of strength and he then ordered an end to the combat.

A few weeks later, I attended the general meeting of the Berkeley Ecumenical Council as an observer, because the by-laws of the council stipulated that only Christian clergy people could be members. I had come in spite of my unsuccessful attempt to rally some moral support for Israel during the war. At the meeting, the board of directors proposed to change the name of the association to the *Berkeley Area Interfaith Council.* They also suggested that the by-laws be modified to allow non-Christian clergy to join the council as full-fledged members and not just as observers. The two measures were unanimously approved and they then proceeded to elect the officers for the following year. They read the names of the nominees for the post of secretary, treasurer and vice-president and when it came to the president, there was a brief moment of silence. The chairman turned toward me and announced that the committee had nominated me to be the next president of the council. I was quite surprised, since I was not even a member of the council fifteen minutes before and had not been asked if I wanted to stand in the first place. They proceeded with the election and the next thing I knew, I had been made the president of the Berkeley Area Interfaith Council. I was amazed by the fact that the very individuals who had refused to sign a petition for peace three weeks before, had now elected me to lead their association.

One of the first projects I helped organize in my capacity as president was a seminar which was jointly sponsored by the National Council of Churches and our association. The National Council's interfaith relations department had requested our cooperation in helping them test some material they intended to use at the convention of the World Council of Churches which was to take place in Nairobi a few months later. They had asked us to invite the leaders of all the religious groups represented in the Bay area to a two-day seminar which would be held at the Tibetan Buddhist Center of Berkeley. This seminar brought together an amazing group of representatives of established Christian denominations, Eastern religions and various cults implanted in the Bay area.

In the evening, while various groups were each presenting a short program by candle-light, a few members of several Eastern religious groups came crawling in the dark toward me to let me know that they were Jewish and had been Bar or Bat Mitzvah or confirmed in a synagogue. There were a number of Jewish Buddhists or "Jew-buds" as we used to call them in the Berkeley idiomatic language of the time, some disciples of Meir Baba and Baba Muktenanda and even some followers of Reverend Sun Myung Moon of the Unification Church. The new cults had become a fad at the time and many Christians and Jews had become involved with their activities, but given the opportunity, they would still acknowledge that they were born Jewish. We examined the texts which the National Council of Churches wanted us to study and offered our comments and feedback to them. The organizers were happy and the Berkeley Council too because this seminar had enabled us to interact together under the same roof for an extended period of time.

As our Sabbath services became more meaningful, we were able to attract more people and many of the visitors to our services indicated their willingness to become members of the congregation. The membership increased by 40% in the first year and continued to grow each following year of my tenure. Within a year, we were able to schedule a Bar or Bat Mitzvah ceremony virtually every other week and conduct our services in the presence of a full house almost every Saturday.

I introduced a new form of participation during the High Holidays services. I invited various members of the congregation to tell us what the holidays meant to them when they were young adults. Some members delivered excellent sermons. All the members of their family and their friends would come to the temple to hear them address the congregation.

As we were approaching the Passover Holiday, I was invited to conduct a Seder at a Presbyterian Church and another one at a Unitarian Church a few days later. Some two hundred members mainly of Jewish descent and others took part in this Passover celebration and I returned year after year for the next seven years. The temple was situated a few blocks away from Le Conte Avenue where six Christian seminaries were located, practically one next to the other. For this reason, the avenue was often referred to as *Holy Hill.* As a consequence, several professors invited me to lecture to their classes from time to time. I was eager to comply with their requests within my ability. I soon became accustomed to speak on a wide range of topics from liturgy to various theological doctrines of Judaism. It happened at a time when a new attitude toward Judaic studies was developing in Christian scholarly circles. The Jewish background of Jesus and the apostles was more freely acknowledged and Christian theologians felt a need to better understand the Jewish context of many passages of the New Testament.

I became involved in a series of interfaith activities with two other clergymen, Rev. George Grose, the Christian chaplain of Whittier College and Dr Muhsen

El Bialy, the Imam of the Islamic Foundation of Southern California. The *Inter-religious Dialogue* had been in existence for several years when I joined it. I succeeded John Rothmann who had been one of the founders of the group. We received some small grants from the Lily Foundation and other foundations which enabled us to organize four or five lecture-dialogues at various universities and seminaries at the end of every month. Rev. Grose was responsible for the planning of our activities. During the following three years, we lectured at over hundred fifty universities and colleges including Harvard University, the Massachusetts Institute of Technology and many other institutions of learning. We had selected half a dozen topics of religious and ethical significance like the belief in monotheism, the pursuit of justice, freedom of choice and determinism, peace in the world. We would each introduce our topic in fifteen minutes and then entertain questions and open a dialogue with the audience. Because our group did not represent only one faith but the three monotheistic faiths, we were invited by academic institutions which might not have invited us otherwise.

We were invited by the *Secretariatus Pro Non-Christiani* (secretariat for relations with non-Christians) of the Vatican which was headed by Cardinal Pignedoli, to come and spend three days in Rome in order to get better acquainted with the inter-religious work done by the Catholic Church. We were also invited by the Executive Secretary of the World Council of Churches in Geneva where a private reception was held in our honor. Our Muslim colleague, Dr Muhsen El Bialy contacted the Mosque of Geneva and it too invited us to attend a Friday prayer service at which time Dr El Bialy was to preach on the theme of inter-religious relations and the work of rapprochement he and his colleagues were doing in the United States. I wrote to the Chief Rabbi of Geneva about our meetings and the Jewish community organized a Friday night dinner in our honor. Everything looked fine until the day before these meetings were to take place. The Imam of the Geneva Mosque called us to let us know that he was canceling our visit to the Mosque because he had received an anonymous telephone call warning him that if I (the Jewish representative) were to enter the mosque, I would not come out of it alive. Concerned with security, the Jewish community followed suit and cancelled the dinner. I had been looking forward to meeting the members of my former congregation and the students I had prepared for their Bar Mitzvah and some of the members of the English Speaking Congregation, but unfortunately, this event did not take place.

Our Muslim colleague had also arranged a visit to Cairo, Egypt which was to follow our Geneva visit. The official invitation issued by the Minister of Religious Affairs of the Egyptian government had arrived just a week before we left California. That visit was not cancelled. We flew to Egypt where we were scheduled to have a meeting with the rector of El Azar University, the foremost Islamic school of theology in the world and several other personalities. This meeting with the rector did not take place, however, because he was engaged in a period of meditation and prayer, we were told. We met with the Minister of Religious Affairs instead and we were invited to participate in the production of a television program which was pre-recorded. All the questions had been carefully prepared by the producers. They asked me several pointed questions like the following,

"Since you believe that all people are endowed with certain inalienable rights, do you think that the rights of the Palestinian people should be respected too?"

"They should, of course," I answered, "all human beings are God's creatures and they all deserve the same respect."

"In that case," the interviewer asked, "don't you think that the Palestinian people are entitled to have their own state, like every other people?"

"Certainly," I said, "the Palestinians deserve to have their own state and it will surely happen as soon as there will be a mutual recognition and peaceful negotiations between the parties involved."

That was one of the statements the reporters were expecting of me. When I watched the program on Egyptian television the next evening, however, I realized that they had edited my statement and that only the first two words of my sentences were heard in English. The voice of a translator was superimposed over mine and only portions of my statements were translated. My mention of "mutual recognition and peaceful negotiations" had been left out altogether. My truncated statement was repeated for weeks on national radio after I left Egypt. When I called the producer and asked for an explanation, she told me,

"I sincerely regret what happened but that was not my fault. I handed over the tape to the editor who abbreviated your statement."

Though it was not my intention to make a political statement, I had been led to make one that was used by the Egyptian Information Office. Two months later, as I joined a delegation of rabbis who went to Israel on a mission, I used that opportunity to meet with the official in charge of relations with Egypt at the ministry of foreign affairs to report on my trip to Cairo. At the time, the Israeli government was not considering the option of helping the Palestinians establish their own state.

My Muslim colleague, Dr El Bialy, became a true friend and I felt affection and respect for him. He would defend moral principles with firmness and courage. When he stated publicly that the slaying of the Israeli athletes at the Munich Olympic games was morally wrong, however, he was immediately dismissed from his post in Los Angeles. He was called to Cairo for consultation and he never returned. His wife was informed that he had died suddenly from a fatal illness.

In the course of my inter-religious activities, I met a young Palestinian student, Shibley Telhami, who was born and raised in Israel. His father had been a high-school principal in a little town near Haifa which had a predominantly Arab population. He was engaged in a program of religious studies at the Graduate Theological Studies which included Islamic studies. When I asked him if his family had been forced to flee Israel during the Independence war, he simply said to me,

"No, we remained in our little town and my father continued to devote himself to education. We were never threatened to leave or expelled from our town."

I then said to him,

"I am glad to learn these facts and I think that other people might be interested to know about them too. If you so desire, I will arrange for you to lecture at various churches in the area. You may also form a team with an Israeli Jewish student so that your message may acquire even greater significance."

I introduced him to Yudit Kornberg, who was an Israeli student at the Graduate Theological Union, and they lectured together for several months. Then, one day, he told me that he had an important meeting with representatives of the Palestinian Liberation

Organization. They had convinced him that their policy was the best for the Palestinian people and he then registered at the University of California to work on a doctorate. Dr Shibley Telhami is today the Anwar Sadat professor for Peace and Development at the University of Maryland and a senior lecturer at the Brookings Institution. Dr Yudit Kornberg-Greenberg is director of the Jewish studies program at Rollins College, Winter Park, Florida.

The news about my activities in the community must have spread across the ocean because I received a telephone call one morning from the president of the *Union Libérale Israélite* of Paris, the only Reform congregation in France at the time. He was urging me to come to Paris for an interview. The congregation sent me a round trip ticket and I got on my way for I could not pass such an opportunity. After several meetings, the members of the executive committee offered me the post of rabbi of their congregation under a special provision. They would hire me in a first stage as an assistant rabbi and give me four months to use all my influence to force the incumbent rabbi to resign, because the congregation was divided over his tenure and because the directors hesitated to terminate his services themselves. I refused to be part of this Machiavellian scheme and I returned to Berkeley. A few months later, an English colleague did just that and the incumbent rabbi resigned after a few months. The unfortunate rabbi fell into a deep depression which lasted for over a year and a half, until some of his followers decided to found a new congregation with him as their rabbi. The new congregation which became known as the *Mouvement Juif Libéral de France* is flourishing today and now surpasses the *Union Libérale* in terms of membership.

Just as I got involved in the Interfaith Council, I became active in the Northern California Board of Rabbis which met once a month. I was also invited to participate in an Inter-religious program *Clergy on the Line* which brought together a Catholic priest, a Protestant minister and a rabbi on KGO, the ABC radio station in San Francisco and I would often serve as the anchor man. During that same period, I was elected president of the Northern Pacific region of the Zionist Organization of America and also president of the San Francisco chapter of the World Conference on Religion and Peace, a non-governmental organization accredited to the United Nations. Even during my vacation time,

I would look for an activity which had some Jewish significance in my eyes.

During my second summer in Berkeley, I organized a project which I called *the Caribbean Mitzvah Corps*. I invited volunteers to join me and my family on the island of St Eustatius, which is near the island of St Maarten, in the Caribbean Sea, to participate in the restoration of the ancient synagogue and the Jewish cemetery which had been abandoned for over hundred years. Statia, as it is called by its inhabitants, was one of the six Caribbean islands of the Netherlands Antilles which were part of the Dutch commonwealth. Spanish and Portuguese Jews had settled on the island at the same time as their brethren in Curaçao, in the early part of the seventeenth century. They had prospered there as international traders until the island was invaded by Admiral Rodney of the British navy during the American War of Independence. He imprisoned all the Jews whom he accused of having helped the American revolutionists in their fight against Great Britain by shipping to them arms and ammunition which they had imported from Europe.

We concentrated our efforts on cleaning up the inside area of the synagogue. I hired a handyman who owned a truck and he took away some fourteen truckloads of garbage from the site until it was completely clean. The roof and the floor of the synagogue had collapsed during a hurricane many years before. All that remained of the synagogue were the walls of yellow bricks which had been imported from Holland after serving as ballast aboard cargo ships. The synagogue had been used as a dumping ground by its neighbors for many years. We made a fence around the ruins of the building and painted signs to indicate that this was the site of Synagogue *H'onen Dalim* (He who is compassionate toward the poor and humble) of St Eustatius. We rededicated this ancient place of worship and we held our first Sabbath service in hundred fifty years. Many of the residents who were watching, were amazed by our devotion to the ruins of this place of worship.

After we completed our task of reclaiming the area of the synagogue, we took upon ourselves to restore the ancient cemetery that had been completely abandoned for over a century. We made rubbings of some of the tombstone inscriptions which were written in Hebrew and in Portuguese. Many of the tombstones, we were told, had been stolen and sold to unscrupulous collectors or had been incorporated in some private houses on the island. One may find a tombstone with the name of the brother of philosopher Baruch Spinoza inscribed on it in one of the old houses of the island.

As I was exploring the area near the cemetery, I became intrigued by the ruins of a small building which might have belonged to the Jewish community at one time and also by a slope that was too smooth to have been a natural characteristic of the terrain. I scratched the ground and I discovered that under the thin layer of earth, there was a paving. It was made of the same yellow bricks that were used in the eighteenth century. As I followed the slope, it occurred to me that it might have been used to collect the runoff water during the rainy season. Indeed, at the bottom of that slope, I found the outline of what had been the *Mikveh,* the ritual bath of the Jewish community. I then called two of my volunteers and we started digging inside the oval basin, removing rocks and dirt from it until it became clear that we had discovered the *Mikveh* of Congregation H'onen Dalim. This was the second ritual bath I had been fortunate to identify in my career. We were now able to establish with certainty that the whole area and the building had belonged to the ancient Jewish community of St Eustatius.

There were only two churches on the island at the time: a Catholic church and a Methodist Church. The minister of the Methodist Church had been transferred a few months before and the congregation had not yet found a replacement. During that time, the elders would conduct services by themselves but they had no one to preach a sermon. After we rededicated the synagogue, they came to me and invited me to give a sermon on the next Sunday which I gladly accepted. They welcomed me with an open heart and I delivered a sermon that was well received. They sang the Lord's prayer on a Calypso tune that was very engaging and I whispered to my neighbor on the pulpit that I loved the melody of the prayer. They must have communicated my reflection with the twinkle of their eyes. The chairman of the board of elders then said at the conclusion of the service that the choir would sing the Lord's prayer one more time to show their appreciation to the guest preacher.

One morning, as my volunteers and I were still busy cleaning up the site of the synagogue, I received a telegram from an attorney in New York requesting that I get in touch with him immediately by telephone. I did not waste any time. I went to the post office and I made my call. The attorney informed me that a group of his clients in the United States were willing to send an important donation to help me with my restoration project. In return, I was to use my influence on their behalf to obtain a permit to build a casino on the island. I answered that I was not the right person to engage in this kind of negotiations. He told me then that I should consider seriously that possibility for it could be beneficial for both of us. Influence peddling, I thought at the time, was not entirely ethical and I refused to get involved in that scheme, but after reflection, I came to the conclusion that it might have been a blessing for the inhabitants of the island who were struggling to make a living. A casino might have provided the jobs that the people on the island thoroughly needed. If I had been a true adventurer, I would have accepted the deal and it would have helped my project and it would have helped the population of the island. In a more modest way, the project of the Caribbean Mitzvah Corps did contribute to the development of tourism on the island.

Back to Berkeley, I resumed my rabbinical and pastoral activities which meant preparing sermons for the High Holidays. The Board of Directors hired an excellent part-time principal who relieved me from the responsibility of supervising the religious school and I felt more at ease with the various facets of my ministry.

After the publication of a Jewish population survey, it became known that the birthrate of the American Jewish community had reached a level that was below the rate of replacement. When I presented the results of this survey to various audiences, there was always a smart fellow who would raise the pointed question,

"Rabbi, what are you doing personally to remedy this situation?"

And I would answer,

"My wife and I already have three children and we may consider increasing our family in the near future. I would like to address my question to you, now: what are you doing about it?'"

In October of that same year, my wife was happy to give birth to twin boys, David and Jonathan. We now had five children or almost three times as many as the average Jewish family in America. We added a room to our house and we had to assume the responsibility for the education of three sons and two daughters.

We entertained friendly relations with our neighbors who lived next door to us. They had a son, Jason, who was of the same age as our son Dan. The boys would often play together. Jason's father was Jewish and his mother was Protestant but this did not prevent him from celebrating virtually all the Jewish holidays with us. When I left the area, I lost track of the family. My children later informed me that Jason had become a member of a skinhead gang. Then, one day, he met a rabbi who convinced him to pursue his studies at Yeshivah University in New York. The outcome was amazing. After several years of study, Jason was ordained as an Orthodox rabbi. He made Aliyah to Israel where he was appointed director of Jewish education in a religious high school in Tiberias in the Galilee. He married the daughter of an American psychiatrist who had settled in Israel and he has a large family today.

Right at the beginning of the school year, the teachers of the Berkeley Unified School District decided to go on strike. After two weeks, a number of parents came to see me to discuss a plan they had conceived. Instead of leaving the children to play in the street with virtually no supervision, they were suggesting that we set up a program for them in the classrooms of the synagogue which would involve some arts and crafts activities and the study of English literature and the Hebrew language. I indicated that I was entirely in favor of such a program and that we should implement it as soon as possible. That was not an easy task, however, because several members of the congregation were strongly opposed to the project on the ground that we should not be scabs during the strike. The two groups of parents were so divided on the issue that in spite of all my efforts, I had to concede that I had been defeated. This matter was very important to university professors who maintained that the right to strike is a sacred right. I was profoundly hurt by the outcome of that controversy and I refused to renew my contract at the end of my five years of service to the congregation.

I could not understand why such a program should be rejected. It was meant to be a temporary measure to keep the children under some supervision while their parents were working. I was burned out. Many members of the congregation begged me to stay on but I would not reconsider. As a consequence, my marriage came under great stress and my wife sought a divorce. It was a painful separation after twenty two years of marriage and after having brought five children into this world. I was heart-broken and it took me several years to overcome this most traumatic experience in my life. I decided to take a sabbatical in France before I resumed my activities.

IX
A RABBI IN A CONVENT

My friends George and Ruth invited me to stay with them in Paris. The Lewineks were managing a home for the aged and taking care of some fifty pensioners. Ruth had been a nurse for many years before she assumed this position. George was assisting her on a part-time basis while he was completing his doctorate in psychology. They extended to me the moral support I needed at this time in my life.

For the Israel Independence Day, I decided to attend the ceremony that took place at the Liberal Synagogue of Beaugrenelle in Paris. At the end of the service, the rabbi let us know that a lecture on Jewish liturgy would be given by a visiting rabbi from London that same evening, only an hour and a half later. As I shook hands with the rabbi, he said to me,

"I may need you tonight to assist the lecturer with some of the translations."

I answered I would gladly do so and would be back in the synagogue for the lecture. As I was leaving the building, I heard a young lady saying that she was also planning to attend the lecture, I then said to her,

"If it is your intention to come back for the lecture, we may have a cup of coffee or tea during the time that is left to us."

She agreed and we walked away from the synagogue. I learned that her name was Myriam Szentes and that she was a native of Hungary. When I asked her what was her occupation, she answered briefly that she was an editorial secretary. When I tried to find out more, she said to me,

"You must wait until we are seated before I tell you more about me."

We entered the first restaurant we found and we ordered some tea and a pizza.

"Now, " I said, "you may tell me who you really are."

"I will probably surprise you," she answered, "but you are entitled to know the truth. I am a nun and part of a religious community."

As I was showing signs of disbelief, she added,

"I am actually the founder of the community and they call me Mother Superior."

"I am not sure whether I should believe you," I said, "but this is fascinating. I never thought I would meet a Mother Superior in civilian clothes in a synagogue."

"There is a simple way of finding out the truth," she added, "you will have to visit me at the convent. We have just acquired a small guest house near the main building and it will be our pleasure to welcome you if you wish to stay with us for a week or two. The sisters will be glad to listen to a rabbi tell them about the main teachings of the Jewish faith."

"Myriam," I said, "I will take you to your word and I will make plans to spend a week at the convent in the very near future."

"The nuns will be allowed to ask questions," she added, "but bear in mind that we abide by the rule of silence unless I give permission to the nuns to speak."

We attended the lecture of Rabbi John Rayner which was well researched. The lecturer did not need much of my assistance for he had an excellent knowledge of French. I said good-bye to Mother Myriam and promised her to see her again at the convent. Two weeks later, I was on my way to Chalons sur Marne where she had agreed to call for me at the railroad station.

Myriam Tunde Szentes was born in Budapest, Hungary. As a teenager, she was a prodigy pianist. Her teachers suggested that she pursue her studies at the prestigious Conservatory of Music of Paris. A year later, after a romantic disappointment, she abandoned her musical studies and she went on a retreat in a convent. She met Father Marie Dominique Philippe who taught philosophy at the University of Fribourg, and she decided to become his student and to work for a doctorate. Seven years later, upon completing a thesis on Aristotelian philosophy and another one on Marxism, she felt a calling to dedicate her life to God. She entered a convent and a few years later, she founded a new religious community which she called *Les Petites Soeurs de l'Immaculée Mére de l'Eglise* (the little sisters of the Immaculate Mother of the Church.) Father Philippe, who had founded the order of *Les Fréres de St Jean* (the Brothers of St John) supported her efforts and helped her find a residence in Rimont, Bourgogne.

When Father Philippe organized a tour to the Holy Land, Sister Myriam joined the group and visited many of the historical sites considered holy by Jews and

Christians. As Myriam was visiting the site of the Tomb of Rachel near Jerusalem, she had a mystical experience which transformed her. After she returned to Europe, she met with her mother who was now living in Geneva, Switzerland and she told her,

"Mother, I have had an amazing experience during this entire tour and especially at the site of the Tomb of Rachel. I felt as if I belonged to the people of Israel."

At that moment, her mother burst into tears and said,

" My daughter, you do belong to Israel. I never told you before that I was Jewish until I converted to Catholicism and that means that we both belong to the people of Israel."

This awareness added a new significance to the personal revelation Myriam had experienced at the Tomb of Rachel. From that day, Myriam declared herself to be Christian and Jewish at the same time and she resolved to work for a rapprochement between the two confessions. She decided to change the name of the community to *Les Soeurs Mariales d'Israel et de St Jean* (the Sisters of Mary, Israel and St John.) At the convent, she endeavored to keep a modicum of Jewish practices. She would light candles on Friday night and recite the *Shema*, the Jewish affirmation of God's unity, in Hebrew, together with the members of the community. She placed a *Mezuzah* at the door of the convent and asked the nuns to wear a Star of David under their habit. Mother Myriam even decided to observe some of the dietary laws and made it a rule for the members of the community to abstain from eating pork meat. She kept these practices because Jesus and Mary had observed them.

When I came to Rimont, Mother Myriam invited me to teach the basic principles of Judaism to the nuns every morning and to answer their questions. In the afternoon, I attended several lectures given by Father Philippe at the monastery of the *Freres de St Jean* which was near-by. I also spent some time discussing ecumenical matters with Mother Myriam and Sister Mary Madeleine who was her faithful assistant. Myriam let me know that her mother had been an executive of the Hungarian Red Cross during the war. She had helped Raoul Wallenberg, the Swedish emissary to Hungary, who saved tens of thousands of Jews in 1944, by issuing them Swedish visas.

After she became familiar with the history of the Jewish state, she started a campaign to demand that the Vatican recognize the state of Israel. Many nations, including the Soviet Union, China and India and even three Arab states had already established diplomatic relations with Israel but the Vatican had not yet done so, forty years after the establishment of the state. She circulated petitions and asked all people of good will to do the same. The recognition by the Vatican did not take place until twenty years later but Mother Myriam was eventually vindicated.

A few months after I returned to America, I invited Myriam to come on a speaking-tour to the United States and I arranged some fourteen lectures, presentations and interviews with the press in Northern and Southern California during the ten days of her stay. I assumed full responsibility for her travel and her accommodation and I also served as her interpreter whenever there was no other person to assume that task. Her personal story made a deep impression on the audiences she addressed and her message was generally well received, though some people were wondering how long the Catholic Church would tolerate her audacious plea for the recognition of the state of Israel.

Her militancy for the cause of a Judeo-Catholicism found some admirers and many detractors. The parents of several nuns who had joined the community and a number of outsiders protested against her religious orientation. After an ecclesiastical trial which took place at the siege of the Lyon bishopric and several investigations by local and national authorities, she was eventually suspended from the Church and her order was dissolved. Three years later, however, Mother Myriam recreated her order and she seemed to be quite happy pursuing her vocation for the greater glory of God and the Roman Catholic Church.

X

A SYNAGOGUE AMID THE WALNUT TREES

Back in California, I accepted a part-time position in Santa Rosa which was only a hour's drive from Berkeley. Congregation Beth Ami presented a new challenge to me. When I first met with Mr. Ben Friedman, the president of the congregation, he was quite pessimistic and he told me,

"Rabbi, we will try to revive this congregation one last time, but if we do not succeed, we will have to disband and terminate our activities. We cannot go on with a small group of some seventy members who do not always show great interest in the congregation."

"Give me a chance," I said, "and I will see what I can do."

I would arrive Friday morning and stay in Santa Rosa until Sunday afternoon. I would visit the sick and give a few private lessons to Bar and Bat Mitzvah candidates on that day. On Friday night, I would conduct a lively service and give a lecture-sermon on a topic of Jewish religious thought which was followed by questions. Since the congregation had not scheduled a Saturday morning service in several years, I organized a short prayer-service on Saturday morning. It was followed by a study-luncheon which attracted some fifteen participants. We were conducting our services in a large classroom from which we could only see an orchard of walnut trees. A few months later, we doubled the size of our study group and we considered moving to the sanctuary. Some of us, however, resisted the idea because our sitting together in a circle had created a feeling of nearness between the members which might be lost in the sanctuary.

I visited many members of the congregation and I met with various people in the community at large who were not yet affiliated with the congregation. The results were most gratifying. We attracted many new members and we went on doubling the size of the membership in one year. At the end of that year, the board of directors offered me to continue my work on a full-time basis. I accepted the offer and I looked forward to a exciting career in this community.

One late afternoon, as I was preparing to leave the library which served also as my office, a young man and his son came to see me. They had come from Sebastopol, a quaint town just a few miles from Santa Rosa. The father explained to me that he was originally from Philadelphia and that he had attended the synagogue of his parents in his youth. When he grew older, however, he had moved away from the Jewish tradition and had become an adept of Buddhism. He had served as the director of the Berkeley Buddhist Center for over twelve years, before he decided to settle in Sebastopol. His son, from a first marriage, was now twelve and a half years old and he wanted him to be Bar Mitzvah. I asked the father,

"Has your son studied some of the essentials of Judaism in a religious school in the years past?"

"Yes," he said, "he attended a Sunday school for a year or two."

"How much time do I have to prepare him?" I asked him.

"Whatever time it will take," he said to me.

I then turned toward the boy and I asked him,

"Are you willing to study for your Bar Mitzvah?"

"Yes," he said, "I am ready to learn whatever is required."

"That is good," I said, "I will meet with you once a week to give you a private lesson. You will have to study by yourself every day and I hope that you will be ready before the end of the year."

We agreed on a schedule of lessons and I started teaching the young fellow. He was always well prepared and knew everything he had been assigned to learn. I asked him a month later,

"You always learn everything that was assigned to you, and I am curious to know how you do that so well. Do you review your lessons with a tutor?"

"No," he said, "I am studying with my father every evening."

"I am very pleased to hear that," I said, "before you leave after your lesson, please tell your father that I would like to talk to him for a minute or two."

A moment later, the father entered the library. I congratulated him for helping his son learn his lessons every night. He then said,

"You see, Rabbi, this preparation gives me a chance to re-learn some of the basic teachings of Judaism I had forgotten or never had a chance to learn in the first place."

I then said to him,

"In that case, I would like to invite you to come to our Saturday morning study-service for you may be interested in the kind of learning which is going on in our group. I remember your telling me you had published several collections of poems a few years ago. With your background, you might be able to help us better understand the meaning of the Biblical texts we are studying together."

He accepted gladly. I gave him a translation of the Jewish Scriptures and showed him the passage we would be studying the following Saturday. He prepared himself and made a brilliant presentation to our group. The participants were so impressed that they decided to invite him again to make another presentation a few weeks later. In due time, Alan Lew became a mainstay of our Saturday morning study-service.

The Bar Mitzvah of his son was a memorable event. Over hundred fifty guests attended the ceremony and the reception which followed. The Bar Mitzvah delivered the sermon which he had prepared with the help of his father. Many of the guests were Buddhist leaders and monks. Several of them had actually been Bar Mitzvah in their youth and had always considered themselves to be Jews even after they became followers of the Buddhist religion.

In the months which followed, Alan and Sherry were married in their home in a Jewish ceremony which I performed according to tradition. When their little girl was born, she was named in their home in the presence of a large group of guests which included many friends of the family. Alan and Sherry were progressively becoming more and more involved in Jewish culture and spirituality. When I left for Paris to attend my mother's funeral and help settle the estate, Alan naturally stepped in and delivered the sermons for the congregation and the study-group. The congregation had come to respect and admire him for his devotion and commitment to the Jewish heritage.

Alan was still working in San Francisco as a tour guide for the Gray Lines Company. One afternoon, as I was in the city to attend a lecture, I happened to meet Alan at Union Square just after he had completed his tour of duty for the bus line. I asked him if he could spare an hour and as he nodded in the affirmative, I invited him to come with me because I wanted to introduce him to the director of the Jewish Community Library. I had read in the Northern California Jewish Bulletin that they were looking for a part-time assistant-librarian. He was interviewed and hired for the position. He was delighted to be able to work for a library which would give him access to scores of books on Jewish wisdom.

I visited the library a month later and I asked Alan if everything was fine. He said to me that he was exhausted and that he had not slept properly in weeks. I asked him what was the cause of his insomnia and he gave me the most unusual reason one could ever think of. He was borrowing many books from the library every day and he would spend the entire night reading them. I then said to him:

"Alan, I think the time has come for you to consider studying for the rabbinate so that you may be able to quench your thirst for Jewish knowledge. The only problem is that we do not have a rabbinical seminary in Northern California and you would have to study for a few years either in New York or Los Angeles."

He was pleased with the idea. We discussed several possibilities and he started the whole process of applying for admission to several seminaries. He was accepted at the Jewish Theological Seminary in New York and he made plans to move with his family. He excelled in all the disciplines he was studying and he received a number of prizes and awards. He spent a year in Israel as required by the seminary and he was ordained as a rabbi a few years later. After three years of service for a congregation in the State of New York, he was elected the rabbi of Temple Beth Shalom, the largest Conservative synagogue of San Francisco. He created a Jewish Meditation Center next to the synagogue and attracted large groups of meditators to various classes and which were scheduled an hour before the regular morning service. He served as president of the Northern California Board of Rabbis. He wrote a book which soon became a best seller *One God Clapping. The Spiritual Path of a Zen Rabbi* in which he narrated the amazing experience which had taken him from Buddhism to Judaism. He remained the spiritual leader of the congregation until he retired a few years ago. He wrote a few more books and he is invited today to lecture all over the country. I am grateful for the fact that Providence had placed me in a position to encourage this talented man to pursue his spiritual quest and eventually find his true vocation.

One morning, I was invited to have lunch with the owner of a winery some twenty miles away from Santa

Rosa. I did not hesitate to accept the invitation. We had lunch in a beautiful rustic salon-dining-room situated in the office building of the winery. I was amazed to find out that the owner was actually a psychologist from New York who had decided, after twenty years of practice, to move to California and get involved in the wine making trade. He had sold his house and all his assets in New York and even cashed in his retirement pension, in order to buy the winery. For years, he had been a member of a wine tasting club and had acquired the basic knowledge of everything pertaining to enology. The idea of producing wine had been part of a dream he had nurtured for many years.

Being from New York, he knew that Orthodox and traditional Jews consumed only Kosher wine at all their celebrations. All he knew was that Kosher wine had to be produced under rabbinical supervision. Now that he owned a winery of some reputation, he was eager to produce a line of Kosher wines too. I told him the basic principles which would have to be followed. I recommended that my predecessor, Rabbi Frankel, who was now the rabbi of a San Francisco congregation, be involved in this matter, because he was ordained as an

Orthodox Rabbi and his supervision might thus be more easily accepted by traditional Jews.

We made plans to observe scrupulously the requirements of Jewish law. The winery hired an Israeli young man to serve as a *mashgiah* (religious supervisor) in the winery, who would be able to ascertain that the wine making had been conducted under proper supervision during the entire preparation, from the squeezing of the grapes to the bottling of the wine.

When the owner of the winery announced in the media that he was about to put on the market Kosher wine produced in his winery, he received an angry letter from a Los Angeles Orthodox rabbi. The letter was informing him that he could not declare his wine Kosher because the California legislators had stipulated a few years before, that only a bona fide Orthodox rabbi could declare that a particular product was Kosher. My colleague had been ordained as an Orthodox rabbi but he was now serving a Conservative congregation and that disqualified him. No one seemed to know about this legal decision in Northern California. The Los Angeles rabbi was not interested in finding out whether we had followed the requirements of Jewish law; his only concern was about the Orthodoxy of the rabbi whose name would appear on the bottle labels. He showed no interest in meeting with us to find out more about the procedure we had followed. His decision was solely based on the fact that the owner of the winery had not hired him - or one of his colleagues – to do the supervision. We were all very disappointed by the extreme rigor of the Orthodox rabbinate, which was determined to keep its monopoly on everything what might be called Kosher in California.

The main reason which had prompted the rabbis of the Talmudic period to require that the making of wine be supervised by a conscientious Jewish person, was to make sure that the wine would not be dedicated to some pagan divinity during its making. In the Middle Ages, several rabbis had acknowledged that this pagan custom was not observed anymore but they hesitated to erase a tradition which had been observed for over two thousand years. They had found a new reason for maintaining it. "Drinking wine with Gentiles," they said, "might lead to inter-marriage and should therefore be forbidden." This experience motivated me once more to fight religious legalism and intolerance within the Jewish community as well as in the community at large.

I pursued my task of attracting new members to my congregation and we soon arrived at the point where we had to consider adding a few classrooms to our building in order to accommodate the increasing number of children who were enrolled in our religious school. A committee was formed to study the feasibility of such a project. The congregation has grown steadily ever since and has become the largest Jewish community center and synagogue in Sonoma county.

Among the active members of the Saturday morning study-prayer session was a retired professor of music who had served as the band leader for General Dwight Eisenhower during World War II. There were some refugees from Germany and also an elderly gentleman and his wife, both natives of Holland, who had spent several years in a Japanese concentration camp in Indonesia during the war. Congregation Beth Ami of Santa Rosa provided the meaningful anchor they had been looking for after the storm.

Though I derived much satisfaction from my rabbinical activities in Santa Rosa, I missed my children whom I could see only on Sunday afternoons. I therefore did not renew my contract with the congregation and I looked for another post which would allow me to spend more time with them. I had contributed to triple the size of the membership of Congregation Beth Ami and I had been instrumental in helping at least one Jewish man not only find his way back to Judaism but to become a rabbi himself.

XI

COUNSELING CRIMINALS

THE CALIFORNIA MEDICAL FACILITY

I became the week-end rabbi of a small congregation in Vallejo and a half-time chaplain at the California Medical Facility, in Vacaville, the largest prison in the state. This arrangement would only require that I spend one night away from home every week. The majority of the members of the Vallejo congregation were retirees and only a few young families had children of school age. They were kind and friendly and eager to maintain the tradition they had received from their parents.

My work at the prison, on the other hand, was extremely challenging and demanding. Though there were only two or three dozen inmates who had declared themselves to be Jewish, I soon became involved with many non-Jewish inmates who were seeking spiritual guidance or personal advice. It was a very large facility where some ten thousand prisoners were detained. A psychiatric hospital was also part of the facility.

MEETING CHARLIE MANSON

A few weeks after I assumed my post at the prison, my inmate secretary whispered to me one morning that Charlie Manson had just arrived, accompanied by two inmate body-guards. I invited him to take a seat while his two friends remained standing.

"I just read your biography in the joint's newsletter," said Charlie Manson, "and I wanted to welcome you in our community."

"That is very kind of you." I said and I asked him, "how should I call you?"

"Just call me Charlie. That's the way most people call me."

"Charlie," I then said, "can I ask you what is the meaning of the swastika that is branded on your forehead? Do you consider yourself a Nazi?"

"No, I am not a Nazi," he answered. "To me, the swastika is a symbol of power and that is why I have adopted it as my emblem."

We then continued our dialogue and I asked him,

"Charlie, would you allow me to ask you a personal question? Do you believe in God?"

"You don't understand, Rabbi," he said with a smile, "I don't have to believe in God. I am God!"

We went on with our conversation in a jovial and serious manner at the same time and I then asked him,

"Do you feel a certain responsibility for other human beings?"

He responded to my question in a composed and incisive way,

"Rabbi, I have to tell you an important fact: no one ever helped me in my growing up and I therefore have no particular obligation toward any one. Those who stand on my way, I simply eliminate."

He then continued,

"Do you think the leaders of this country and its government are acting in responsible ways when they keep destroying the environment and the ecology of this world? They surely do not seem to care about the future of humanity. So why should I?"

"Charlie," I said. "many great projects have been realized by people of good will who dedicated themselves to a task they believed in. They were not always people in government positions. You could be one of them. You certainly have the leadership skills that are required."

"You are forgetting, Rabbi," he said immediately, "that they are keeping me in this joint because they don't like the way I do things."

"You know, Charlie," I answered, "there are several guys who are doing amazing things right here in this place."

"I am not ready to become an altar-boy," he said, "it's not in my nature."

I was following his train of thought. I was not trying to probe his criminal mentality or ask him why he had committed violent crimes in the past. He must have thought I was quite naive but at the same time he must have felt flattered by some of my compliments.

Charlie came to see me regularly for the next two years. He always had a topic or two he wanted to discuss with me. During these conversations, he told me many facts about his past life and about his interaction with the authorities. I learned that his mother was barely sixteen years old when he was born. She was working in a bar to support herself and she had little time to care for her child whom she eventually abandoned. The boy was placed in various homes and institutions from which he would often escape. He would be re-captured by the police and sent to another foster-home. He felt that no one had ever paid much attention to him and that he had grown up by himself. On one occasion, he told me,

"If I had not believed that I had the power of a god, I would never have been able to survive the rotten childhood I had."

Charlie had just a few years of schooling and could barely read and write, but he had great charisma and a natural disposition for theatrical effects. He would often ask me to meet him in the interdenominational chapel rather than in my small office. He would then re-arrange the chairs and set the stage before he spoke to me. I would listen and only interrupt him to ask for more information. I never formally condemned the crimes he had committed. I would only ask him to explain to me why he had done these things. That is probably why he would come back once or twice a week, when he was not locked up in a solitary cell.

When he was in seclusion, I would visit him in his cell from time to time. The guard would open the door, let me in and lock the wrought-iron door behind me. He would then instruct me to call him when I had finished my visit so that he might open the door to let me go. Charlie was aware that I was nervous when I was locked up with him in his narrow cell and he would sit at the other end of the bed during our conversation.

One day, after he was allowed to return to his dormitory, he came to see me in an angry mood. He wanted to let me know that a certain New England attorney would be severely punished if he did not stop asking too many questions of one of his friends, a young lady who lived in the Boston area. She was trying to negotiate a contract with a record company for the commercial production of a tape containing songs he had composed. The cassette had been smuggled out of the prison and handed over to this woman. He gave me the phone number of the attorney and said that I should warn him immediately about the situation because *Ice pick* might otherwise intervene. Considering the gravity of such a threat, I went home and I called the attorney. The warden of the prison later informed me that I should not have contacted the attorney but that I should have informed him or the FBI about the threat. I learned my lesson and became more circumspect before I did anything for an inmate or their friends.

I organized a few study groups on various religious topics with some degree of success. When I announced, however, that I would be giving an introductory class in the Hebrew language, I was amazed by the response. Over one hundred inmates signed up for the class. Since the majority of them were not Jewish, I wondered why they were so eager to learn an ancient language like Hebrew. When I asked them the reasons that had motivated them, I was flabbergasted by their answers. Many of them thought that the knowledge of Hebrew was a contributing factor to the intelligence and ability of the Jewish people they had known in the past and that by learning Hebrew, they were hoping to acquire some of the virtues they had admired in Jews. I taught them to read and write Hebrew and even to write coded messages in Hebrew which they thought was quite a cool way of communicating without being caught by the guards or so they thought.

As we were about to celebrate Passover, the Festival of Freedom in Jewish tradition, I got a similar response: over hundred twenty inmates signed up for the *Seder*, the special dinner which is preceded by the reading of the biblical story of the Exodus from Egypt. A number of guards and officers joined us at our festive meal which was brought in by a Jewish caterer from San Jose. He was a survivor of the holocaust and he still remembered how starved he had been in the Nazi concentration camps. After he was freed by the Allies, he made a vow that he would provide food to prisoners when the opportunity would present itself. He had chosen this way to express his gratitude to the Creator who had helped him survive the hunger and misery he had endured in the camps. On our Passover Seder, virtually all the inmates identified with the Hebrews of the Bible and they must have prayed for their liberation from incarceration.

MEETING EDMUND KEMPER

One evening, I got extremely scared and afraid for my life. It was six o' clock. My Catholic and Protestant colleagues had already left for the day and I was about to close my office, when an extremely agitated inmate arrived and asked if he could speak to me. I went back into my office and I invited him to take a seat. He was a very tall and strong man and I realized immediately that I could not have done anything to defend myself if he had attacked me. I would not have been able to reach the alarm button, because he sat right in front of my desk. I already anticipated the worst possible scenarios. He could have gagged me and even killed me, taken my clothes, my ID and my badge and tried to escape from the prison. He could have locked me up in that small office, cut the telephone wire and dismantled the alarm system and no one would have known what happened to me until the next day. I soon realized, however, that this was not the intention of my visitor. He introduced himself; he was Edmund Kemper. I did not know exactly who he was, but he knew who I was, because he had seen me many times walking in the corridors of the facility. He said,

"Rabbi, you would not believe what just happened to me. I spoke to my father for the first time in twenty years. He is dying of cancer in a hospital, but we were able to talk like father and son as we had never done before. I submit to you that if my father had spoken to me that way when I was a teenager, I would not be here today. I would not have done what I did."

He spoke to me for over an hour.

"I am very sensitive to everything you told me," I said, "I am glad you had the opportunity to reconcile with his father. This conversation must have brought moral healing to both of you."

We decided to meet again in the following days. I went to the law library the next day and I learned that he had killed ten people including his grandparents, his mother and a friend of hers and six female students before he finally turned himself in to the police. He would have received the death penalty but the citizens of the state of California had just approved a measure to abolish it. Instead he was condemned to several hundred years of incarceration. Unlike the other serial murderers I had met in the facility, Kemper had experienced a complete change of heart. He had expressed regret for what he had done after he started serving his prison sentence. He was now trying, albeit in a very small way, to "repay society" for the crimes he had perpetrated. He had obtained the permission from the prison authorities to undertake a humanitarian project within the walls of the institution. Together with a few other inmates, and a small grant from a foundation, he was making cassettes for the blind. He said to me facetiously,

"I may say without exaggeration, that I am the best read man in this whole facility."

Edmund Kemper was resigned to the fact that he would spend the rest of his life behind bars and he was not angry and resentful about it. He had found a certain peace of mind after he adopted an Eastern philosophy whose teachers were corresponding with him on a regular basis.

All these experiences enabled me to better understand the mentality of the various groups of prisoners. I learned that there were white collar breakers of the law and violent criminals. Among the inmates I was counseling, was a former professor of psychiatry at a prestigious university in California who had been sentenced to several years of prison for cheating on the health insurance claims he was submitting to the head office. He would falsely state that he had seen a patient three times when he had seen him only once. He had conceived this scheme in order to provide the extra money his wife needed to buy the illegal drugs to which she was addicted. A year after he had been imprisoned, he still felt no remorse and would not admit that he had committed a crime by doing what he did. He eventually lost his license to practice in California and he probably moved to another state when he was released from prison.

My first inmate secretary was an attorney who had been at the service of Jimmy Hoffa, the head of the Teamsters Union, who had disappeared one day without leaving any trace. He organized my appointments with great diligence and always prepared the material I needed for my classes. He would only ask for the favor to make a telephone call to the outside from time to time. I soon realized he was using my office to give legal consultations to some of the inmates. When I reported the fact to the warden, he gave me permission to let him continue doing so within reason. He had been found guilty of a typical white collar crime. He had applied for several loans from various banks by using the same property as collateral. The banks had eventually found out about the scheme and he was sentenced to one year of detention in a state correctional institution.

"I wish to explain to you, Rabbi," he said to me when I first interviewed him for the job, "that I had no intention of stealing the money I borrowed; I was repaying the banks according to schedule."

On another occasion, he told me how he discovered, that his father had been a bookmaker all his life.

"I was fifteen years old. My father had just died and we were observing the *Shivah* (the days of mourning) for him when my father's private phone rang. I answered the call. At the other end, I heard a man say: 'Hello, Harry, I want to place a bet on the champion, number 86. Put me down for $2000. I will call you to-morrow.' I did not have a chance to tell the caller that Harry, my father, had just died three days before and that we were reciting memorial prayers for him when he called."

After he was released from prison, another inmate applied for the job. He was a trans-sexual fellow who had already undergone the first operation which would make him a woman but he was still regarded as a man by the prison authorities. He was accused of having stolen the car of a friend but he claimed that his friend had given him permission to use his car. He was respectful and affectionate and appreciated the fact that he was working for the Jewish chaplain.

He never mentioned anything about his father but he told me about the strange relationship he had with his mother. When he was barely seven years old, his mother became exceedingly upset one day, when he dressed up like a little girl. His mother took him to a psychiatrist for she suspected some abnormality in his behavior. The boy was then placed in a children's home where he underwent a program of re-education. He was then allowed to return to his family, but his mother's fear never abandoned her. She was afraid that her son might still manifest the inclination of wanting to be a girl. By the time he reached the age of majority, he formally declared his intention to have a sex-change operation. I asked one of the psychiatrists who worked at the facility what he thought of this case. He answered me that it was virtually impossible to ascertain whether he had been the victim of a particularly obsessed mother or whether his genetic make up was responsible for his desire to identify as a person of the other sex. I could not help but think that if he had been brought up by a loving mother and treated by a competent psychiatrist, he might have grown up to be a happy young man.

I would not have been able to cope with the responsibilities of my job without the help of my supervisor in marriage and family counseling. He was a former Catholic priest of Irish descent who had left the priesthood in order to get married. He had earned a doctorate in clinical psychology and received a degree in marriage and family counseling. His keen insight and moral support helped me fulfill my obligations as a prison chaplain.

On another occasion, a talented man in his forties came to see me and asked for some guidance. He expected to be released two weeks later and he was perplexed about what he might do in the world outside. I asked him:

"What is it that you love doing and can do best?"

"That is simple," said the fellow, "what I can do best is forging documents."

"Tell me more about it." I said.

"Rabbi, it's very simple. There are a number of bars in San Francisco where you can buy stolen checks at a nominal price. If you are daring, you purchase a few checks in the amount of $10,000 or more. You go home and you create a driver's license with the name of the person on the check and your picture affixed to it. It is not a difficult task especially if you can manage to get some blank forms from the Department of Motor Vehicles at a low price. I then go to a bank where no one knows me and I ask to open a new account. I present my new driver's license and I start filling in the application. When the clerk asks me how much money I would like to deposit in my account, I present the check that corresponds to the ID and I sign it. The clerk thanks me for patronizing his bank. I shake hands with him and before I take leave of him, I ask him when the check will be cleared. At the due date, I go back to the bank to cash in the value of the check and I go out quickly from the bank and disappear with the money. I can repeat that scheme some fifteen or sixteen times on average before I get caught. During that time, I live very well and do all kinds of exciting things. I know all along I am taking a risk by doing these things. When I am arrested, I am usually sentenced to one or two years in prison and that is not too bad."

"Why don't you apply for as job with the FBI or a bank?" I said to him, "it would seem that your ability to detect forgeries might be appreciated and you might thus render a service to the community."

"Oh, no," he said, "I would never do such a thing. That would be no fun at all."

"You don't know until you give it a try. You may feel at peace with yourself as you have never felt before. You surely do not want to come back to this place once again. Do you?"

"I will tell you frankly, Rabbi," he answered, "I have not yet come to that point. I am not yet ready to change my habits and become a regular fellow. My game, at this stage, consists in beating the system. May be, one day..."

"When you hear the voice of your conscience speak to you, you will have to act upon it. You cannot avoid the real issues for the rest of your life."

"I understand what you say, Rabbi, and I have no doubt that I will probably come to that realization one day, but for the time being, I will do what I can do best..."

"You can do better than break the law, my friend," I said, "but you must give it a chance and be courageous."

"Rabbi, if you were to try it, you would understand what I mean. Would you like me to teach you my modus operandi just to get a sense of the excitement you may derive from it?"

"No, thank you," I said, "I appreciate your friendship and your willingness to teach me your skills. I am convinced that you have the make-up of an honest man and I am not giving up hope on you. Good luck in your life ahead!"

I had done my best to help him think about the possibility of leading a decent life outside the institution. In my experience with inmates, I had discovered that most of them had given some thought about abandoning their mischievous ways and becoming law abiding citizens but they had not found the courage to make the new decision.

When I would come back home after a long day spent at the prison, I was glad to return to the real world. I would then think about my dear ones, my children and my friends and resolve to show to them the same solicitude and love I had felt for criminals. I would call my children and make some plans to see them within the limitations of my visitation rights. Even though the court had decided I should have joint custody, my ex-wife objected to my having my younger children stay with me more than the prescribed weekend every other week. I was not allowed to take my children to Europe during their summer vacation period because they would be away from her supervision.

I was so frustrated by this restrictive access to my children that I gave up the fight. I left to my ex-wife the responsibility of educating the twins the way she thought best. I decided to take a rabbinical post in South Africa where there were five Progressive congregations looking for a rabbi.

XII

IN THE LAND OF APARTHEID

I arrived in Johannesburg in October 1987 in order to join a team of rabbis who were ministering to three Progressive synagogues. My main assignment was to Temple David in Sandton, a Northern suburb of Johannesburg, which was in the process of becoming a new residential and financial center for the white middle-upper class population.

The members of my congregation assumed that I was well informed about the patterns of living in the country and they did not deem it necessary to brief me about some of the peculiar mores of the land. Since I was without a car during the first three weeks, I depended upon the good will of several volunteers to take me to the various places I had to go; and when none was available, I used public transportation.

The first time I took a public bus, I had quite an unusual experience. As I was about to step up on the bus which would take me from Oxford Road to Sandton, the driver told me,

"Not for you, Master."

"But you are going to Sandton, aren't you?"

"Yes, but this bus, not for you." said the driver.

I did not understand what he was trying to tell me and I got up anyway and looked for an empty seat. As I was about to sit down, I realized what the driver had been trying to convey to me with great tact. All the passengers in the bus were black. They were quiet and would not even raise their eyes to look at me for I was a stranger among them and they probably thought I was either a government agent or some suspicious individual. This bus was indeed a bus reserved for black people. I did not know at the time that there were also buses for white people.

That was my first encounter with the racial discrimination of the apartheid regime. Though some of the legal restrictions were beginning to disappear, the buses were still segregated. The South African white residents did not like to speak to foreigners about these matters because they were too embarrassing.

The members of my congregation had no reason for feeling guilty about the official racial policy. They were doing their share to fight it and bring a small measure of social justice in their immediate vicinity. They had organized a *Mitzvah School* for some eighty or ninety high-school seniors of the nearby black township of Alexandra. The school was housed in what used to be the rabbi's house, right in the middle of the synagogue campus.

Two private buses were hired by the committee in order collect the students every morning, bring them to the school and take them back every evening. Several volunteers from the congregation and several paid part-time teachers would conscientiously provide an intensive preparation for the *matriculation* examination which would allow them to register at any university. Those who needed special help would receive individual tutoring. The results were amazing. Whereas only 20% of the township high school seniors were able to pass the exam, the students enrolled in the Mitzvah School had a 75% rate of success. This was accomplished in just one year of intensive study.

The synagogue was build in the form of a *rondavel,* a circular hut covered with thatch which served as a dwelling to most indigenous people living in the countryside. It had large windows all around from which we could see the luxuriant trees of the garden on all sides. For the High Holidays, we would open the back panels of the synagogue and attach an enormous tent to accommodate the crowd which attended services on these occasions.

Most of the members of the congregation were second or third generation descendants of the Jews who had immigrated from Lithuania for the main part. They were now acculturated to the South African way of life. We had a Bar/Bat Mitzvah ceremony every other week which would attract many visitors and friends. It was usually followed by a lavish reception in the gardens surrounding the synagogue or in a private country club. Some of our critics used to call our synagogue a *Bar Mitzvah Mill*. The preparation and the celebration of these family events was one of my responsibilities.

Besides my religious and pastoral duties, I taught several classes for adults including an Introduction to Judaism class which was attended by some twenty married couples or individuals who were planning to convert to Judaism. I also taught classes at the other congregations which were part of our association of Progressive synagogues.

After a lecture at Temple Emmanuel, I met Rosemary June Epstein, who was an active member of the congregation and who had served as a board member at one time. She was of Lithuanian descent as were my grandparents. A friendship developed between us and we eventually decided to get married. The ceremony took place at her Temple in the presence of many guests and members of our respective congregations.

The agreement between our three Progressive congregations provided that a family affiliated with one of them could use the facilities of the other two congregations if they so desired. Members of our sister-congregations would often request the privilege of holding their reception in the facilities of our campus. When my colleague of Temple Emanuel brought his own choir to Temple David one Sunday afternoon to officiate at the wedding of one of his members, the choir of my synagogue was extremely upset. They resigned in protest because they had not been invited to sing at the ceremony. Contrary to their expectations, however, the congregation accepted their resignation. After four weeks without a choir, my wife Rosemary became the choir director. She was a fine musician and had been singing in synagogue choirs ever since she was eight years old. She recruited a new team of singers and she prepared them to perform during the Sabbath services. We were thus conducting services together and this joint participation added a spiritual dimension to our marital relationship.

Since we had no religious service on Saturday afternoon, I would attend the *Minh'ah* (afternoon) service at an Orthodox synagogue. I was always welcomed by the participants and often given the honor of being called to the Torah as if I had been a regular member. My presence, however, must have caused some unhappiness to some members of the community at large who thought that Progressive Jews should not be allowed to participate in an Orthodox service. Some of these critics reported the fact to the members of the *Beth Din* (Orthodox religious council) and asked for a ruling.

Rabbi Moshe Kurstag, the head of the Beth Din, was a Talmudic scholar who had studied in the traditional *Yeshivot* (religious academies) of Lithuania. In his eyes, the members of Progressive and Conservative congregations were utterly misguided and were to be placed in the same category as apostates. This issue took on an additional importance because one of my colleagues, Rabbi Arthur Seltzer, of Temple Israel of Cape Town, also attended an Orthodox synagogue on a regular basis. He too was being called to the Torah and was invited to conduct the service from time to time. The learned rabbis of the Johannesburg Beth Din considered the matter and decided that this practice was contrary to the requirements of Jewish law and should be forbidden. They sent a pastoral letter to all the synagogues affiliated with the United Synagogues of South Africa to inform them that no Progressive rabbi should be called to the Torah in a God-fearing Orthodox congregation.

I felt as if I had been condemned by the tribunal of the Inquisition without any due process. The members of the Beth Din had ruled that my colleague and I were not to be considered legitimate members of the Jewish community. We were to be treated as if we were renegades, like Uriel Da Costa and Baruch Spinoza, the two Jewish thinkers who were excommunicated by the Amsterdam Beth Din, for having failed to observe all the details of Jewish law after they formally returned to Judaism. In Amsterdam, however, they were summoned by the Beth Din and given a chance to recant. In South Africa, the staunch defenders of the Jewish faith had condemned us without even knowing who we were. Those seemingly learned rabbis had passed a sentence on fellow Jews with the same severity and intolerance as their misguided predecessors of the seventeenth century.

All this happened while the overwhelming majority of South African Jews were very lax in matters of religious observance and many transgressed the norms of Orthodox Judaism. Most of those who attended synagogue services on Saturdays, drove their automobiles and left their vehicles in the parking lot of the synagogues under the watchful eyes of the employees of the congregation who had been hired for that purpose. Against this background of non-compliance to the requirements of Jewish law, the Beth Din was still deciding on these matters as it would have done in the nineteen century in Lithuania.

A few months after the publication of this pastoral letter, I had another run up with the Johannesburg Beth Din which caused me much pain and sadness. It happened as a consequence of a marriage ceremony which I performed. A couple had requested that I officiate at their wedding. The bride was a gracious lady of Afrikaner background who had just converted to Judaism in Switzerland. I did not know that the bride, Ms Anneline Kriel, had been crowned as Miss South Africa and then Miss Universe a few months later. The groom, Phillip Tucker, was a member of a wealthy Jewish family that had lived in the country for many years. Ms Kriel showed me her conversion certificate which was signed by Rabbi Mordecai Piron, the former Chief Chaplain of the Israeli Army, who had taken a post in Zurich, Switzerland, upon retiring from the military chaplaincy. She also handed to me a letter from the office of the Chief Rabbinate of Israel stating that the conversion had been accepted and that the marriage could take place in Israel at any time. I called Rabbi Piron in Switzerland and he confirmed to me that the conversion had been completed according to Halakhah (Jewish law).

As I was wondering why they had asked me to officiate, they explained to me that they were to be married by Rabbi Nachman Bernhard, the respected rabbi of the Oxford Synagogue in Killarney, who was a friend of the groom's family. However, the rabbi had just informed them that he would not be able to officiate because the Beth Din of Johannesburg would not recognize the validity of her conversion to Judaism on the pretext that it was performed outside of South Africa.

The marriage was performed with great pomp on the grounds of the groom's family mansion. Hundreds of guests and family members attended the event which was largely covered by the local press and television. I observed the traditional ritual and all the customs of the South African communities. From the moment the marriage was announced, however, all kinds of malicious rumors began to spread in the community. I received many insulting calls and even death threats from callers who refused to identify themselves. They objected to the fact that I was prepared to officiate at a wedding even though the bride's conversion was not valid. They had been told by the rabbis that this was a desecration of Judaism and they would have stopped me from performing the ceremony if they had been able to. Local newspapers got involved in the controversy and my stay in the country became so unpleasant that I considered the possibility of leaving South Africa.

In my own congregation, I was confronting another unpleasant situation which affected my relationship with the president of my congregation. Under the strong influence of a *Chabad-Lubavitch* rabbi who strongly opposed the Progressive ideology, my president became convinced that we were not doing the right things and he started blaming me for my liberal and tolerant attitude. Nothing I was doing was good enough anymore because it was not done the Orthodox way. After months of internal bickering with me and the board of directors, he eventually left Temple David to join the *Chabad Schul* whose rabbi had become his spiritual mentor.

In order to avoid being consumed by these congregational quarrels, I turned to the community at large and got involved in several cultural activities which brought me great satisfaction. I took the initiative of teaching courses and seminars in Logotherapy under the auspices of the Viktor Frankl Foundation of South Africa and an introductory course to the Yiddish language under the auspices of the extension department of the Witwatersrand University in Johannesburg. I also gave a series of lectures on Kabbalah and Medical Ethics which were extremely well received.

One Friday night, basing my remarks on the prophetic reading of the week, I gave a sermon on the Jewish attitude toward the resurrection of the dead and

I announced at the end of the services, that I would speak on spiritism and necromancy the following Friday. Many people I had never seen before came to hear the sermon. Most of them, I learned later, were members of a Johannesburg group involved in spiritism. The two leaders of the group, a Jewish psychologist and a Christian psychic, were in the audience. They invited me to meet with them to further discuss the topic of spiritism. We met several times but I declined their invitation to join the group.

A few weeks later, as I was attending a lecture in an Orthodox synagogue, I was amazed to read a pastoral letter on psychic practices posted on the bulletin board of the congregation. It was issued by the Johannesburg Beth Din and signed by its president, Rabbi Kurstag. He was warning the members of the community that it was strictly forbidden, according to Jewish law, to practice necromancy and participate in séances during which the spirit of the dead was invoked, as King Saul had done in his days - as is related in the second book of Samuel. I was intrigued by the fact that they were so well informed about everything that was happening in my synagogue. I suspected that some of our members - or just one of them - must have been so concerned about the salvation of their soul that they would immediately report to the Beth Din any activity that they thought was not in keeping with traditional Judaism. When I tried to make an appointment with a leading Orthodox rabbi, he politely declined to meet with me.

While some social and political changes were taking place in South Africa, many members of the Jewish community were leaving the country in search of a new home. Many of them emigrated to Australia, Great Britain or Canada. Few made *Aliyah* to Israel because they were afraid of terrorism. As some put it, "it would make no sense to go out of the frying pan into the fire."

My wife and I eventually decided to follow their example and we returned to the United States. During the near four years I spent in the country, I witnessed the political evolution which brought the *apartheid* regime closer to an end.

XIII
A CONSERVATIVE CONGREGATION IN CALIFORNIA

Back in the United States, I did not want to serve as the rabbi of another congregation. I applied for a State license to practice marriage and family counseling and looked for a position which would enable me to complete my internship. When I saw an ad in the Northern California Jewish Bulletin of a congregation seeking for a rabbi in Long Beach, I was unable to control my reaction. I called the president of Temple Beth Shalom and he invited me to have an interview with the rabbi's search committee. I spent a week-end with the congregation and I was offered a two year contract. My wife and I then moved to Long Beach and we bought a house near the synagogue. I was ready to assume my new responsibilities.

Temple Beth Shalom was only twenty five years old. It was established at a time when middle-class people were moving away from the downtown area toward more residential suburbs. A physician, who served on the board of a downtown congregation, had taken the initiative of starting the new project. He invited a number of his colleagues and friends to join him in order to create a new congregation in the Bixby Knolls area of Long Beach. Many followed him in his new venture and that explained why such a large number of physicians were part of its membership.

The congregation thrived during the first fifteen years of its existence until it was severely affected by a new shift in population. Many families with school-aged children were now leaving the area because of the high crime-rate in the city. Even the schools were not safe any more. Metal detectors had to be installed at the entrance of the main high-school and police patrol cars were parked in front of the building most days. The congregation lost many of its young families. The religious school dwindled in size and was compelled to merge with the school of the near-by Lakewood congregation, which was suffering from the same attrition. A potential merger of the two congregations was considered but after many years of a prolonged dialogue between the leaders of the two temples, no decision had been reached. The Lakewood congregation claimed to be more traditional than the Long Beach one; they would not allow women to be called to the Torah. Several years later, however, the Lakewood group engaged a Reform rabbi on a part-time basis, but the merger between the congregations still did not take place.

The members of Temple Beth Shalom seemed to be satisfied with the tradition they had adopted at the time of its inception and they were not looking for any major change. Even a simple matter like allowing people to sit wherever they wanted on the High Holidays, was not approved by the Board of Directors after four consecutive sessions during which that question was debated. The seats were assigned by the ritual committee and the executive secretary of the synagogue. As a consequence, the first three rows in the sanctuary often remained empty on the High Holidays because they had been allocated to the older members of the synagogue who did not attend services very often, except on the eve of Yom Kippur and the *Yizkor* Memorial prayer on the following day.

I conducted services with a fine gentleman who served as a part-time cantor. All week long, he was busy managing his accountancy firm but on the Sabbath he would devote himself to his true avocation which was singing in the synagogue. At festive celebrations, he would always sing a number of arias from various operas which delighted the congregation.

All went well until his seven year-old son died suddenly from a severe asthma attack. The man changed completely and nothing could alleviate his pain and sorrow. He went to pray at the graveside of his son every day, for a whole year and even after. At the cemetery, he met another couple of grieving parents who were disconsolate for having lost a teenage son. They became friends and they suggested he consult a team of psychics who had helped them *communicate* with their son. The bereaved father followed their advice and met with the two practitioners of the occult *science*. They made him believe that they had been able to reach his son in the other world and that he was doing well. The distressed father put his trust in those *mediums* and would not listen to any one who would suggest that they only pretended to communicate with his departed son. This awkward situation caused a great tension in his family and within a short time, the cantor went through a painful divorce. The sudden death of his son had so deeply traumatized him that he was unable to recover from the suffering he was experiencing. The members of the congregation and his friends did not spare their love and sympathy for him but he remained impervious to their kindness and he eventually resigned from his post at the synagogue.

The religious school was supervised by a small committee of parents and administered by a principal who was a secular Israeli woman who had served in the army in her country but was in no way a religious educator. As a result, the children did not learn much about the Jewish faith or even the Hebrew language. They attended classes reluctantly in order to comply with the requirements set up by the congregation for anyone wishing to have a Bar/Bat Mitzvah ceremony in the synagogue. Following the routine practiced in many congregations, the teenagers were expected to chant a page or two of the Hebrew text of the weekly reading from the Prophets and prepare a little address which would be delivered during the service. The ceremony would be followed by a reception and a separate party for the teenagers in many cases. On one occasion, the parents of the Bat Mitzvah invited some two hundred guests to a lavish banquet which took place in the salons of the Queen Mary ship which had been retired from service and was now moored in the Long Beach harbor.

When Michael Fishman was Bar Mitzvah, the synagogue was full to capacity. The young Michael had been a member of the cast of the Roseanne television show for several years and was well-known to most television viewers. In order to honor the young actor, Roseanne Barr came to Temple Beth Shalom to attend the ceremony.

When the parents of a few boys between the age of twelve and thirteen who had never attended a religious school before, met with the school committee and requested that their sons be Bar Mitzvah, they were told that they must attend the school for three years as was specified in the by-laws of the school. This would have deferred their Bar Mitzvah to the age of sixteen. I was unable to convince the committee members to take a more conciliatory stand on this issue to allow the boys to celebrate their Bar Mitzvah at an earlier date. The committee insisted on maintaining the by-laws of the school and its chairman said to me at the time:

"You don't have to love it, but you must obey the rule."

Disregarding the decision of the committee, however, I took upon myself to prepare the boys for their Bar Mitzvah by giving them private lessons. The youngsters did not attend the religious school but they put their heart into their studies and were the only teenagers who attended the Saturday morning services regularly. One of these boys had to convince his parents that he wanted to be Bar Mitzvah. He was an intelligent and kind-hearted boy who had one day, when he was ten years old, saved the cleaning lady working for his family from drowning in their swimming pool. He was then invited to the White House to receive a special medal of valor from the president of the United States.

I had brought to the attention of the members of the committee the results of several research studies which indicated that a majority of the pupils attending late afternoon religious school classes were often turned off by the mediocre quality of the teaching offered. Several leading researchers had even concluded that far from strengthening the Jewish identity of the children, these classes constituted a liability for the Jewish community. The school committee and its chairman dismissed these facts as irrelevant. The quality of the educational system was not their concern. They were just applying the rules.

Realizing that the Religious School students were not attending services, I asked Louise Marak, a member of the congregation, to organize children's services on Saturday mornings and she was able to attract and motivate a large number of them. She later created a little prayer-book which was also used by the adult congregation from time to time, and we all took pride in her accomplishments.

The only two children who came regularly to services every Saturday morning were the two daughters of Michael Natelson, a faithful member of the congregation who never missed a service. He was married to Annie who had converted to Judaism before they got married. These two girls knew all the prayers by heart and would always walk with their father as he was carrying the Torah scroll and they would sing with him when he was saying the Mussaf (additional prayer) of the Sabbath service. It was a pleasure observing them following in the footsteps of their father's religious tradition.

After two years of service to the congregation, I applied for membership with the Rabbinical Assembly of the Conservative movement. I was invited for an interview in New York and I was later informed that they would accept me as a member on condition that I resign from the Reform association. I complied with the wishes of my colleagues, even though it did not make much sense to me. At the time, an interesting phenomenon was taking place within the two movements. Whereas the Conservative movement was becoming more liberal, the Reform movement was in the process of reintegrating some of the traditional rituals it had discarded one hundred years earlier. These significant transformations had led the Chancellor of the Jewish Theological Seminary, Dr Ismar Schorsch, to declare in his retirement address, a few years later:

"The Conservative movement is becoming a Reform movement and the Reform movement is becoming Conservative."

In virtually all matters of Jewish observance, the Conservative organization would usually keep pace with the bold initiatives of the Reform movement. When the Reform decided to ordain women or gay and lesbian rabbis, the Conservative movement strongly rejected this measure. And then, a few years later, it made the same decision. The only difference between them was their stance on intermarriage, though many Conservative rabbis had simplified the conversion process to the point of becoming a mere formality.

The Introduction to Judaism class always attracted Jewish and non-Jewish students eager to learn about Judaism. On one occasion, however, I encountered a most embarrassing situation. I had just stated that one should only convert if he/she was convinced that Judaism was the best religion for him/her and for no other reason. At that moment, a young lady, who was one of the students in the class, burst into tears and started sobbing. She and her fiance left the classroom so as not to disturb the other students. I finished my class and went back home. As I opened the door, the telephone was ringing and I received a dozen calls one after the other. The parents of the Jewish man who was engaged to the young lady, their friends and a member of the board of the congregation, were all asking me to apologize to the young lady for my "rude" remarks. I had offended a lovely person who had kindly agreed to go through all these motions for only one reason: to marry the Jewish man whom she loved. They all told me that it was out of love that she was attending the class and not out of conviction. They asked me to find a way of repairing the damage I had caused by my 'lack of sensitivity.' After listening to all these requests, I arranged for the couple to meet with a colleague and friend of mine who was affiliated with the Reform movement and he performed the wedding without asking too many questions.

One of the elders of the congregation told me at the time,

"Rabbi, you cannot expect deep-religious convictions from a person who has only one purpose in mind: to marry a Jewish man."

I had then answered,

"Conversion is the expression of a conviction and an act of faith in the sight of God and not a formality. The couple could have been married in a civil ceremony and the young lady would not have had to violate her conscience in order to please her husband and her in-laws."

This elderly gentleman was probably trying to convey to me the fact that many Jews in America felt closer to their ethnic and cultural legacy than to their religious and spiritual heritage and that the young lady was aware of this phenomenon. I learned with great amazement that the young man was elected president of the congregation a few years later and that his wife became involved in all the social and communal activities of the synagogue.

One Sunday morning, the Men's Club of the synagogue invited Professor Robert Eisenman from California State University in Long Beach, to lecture on the Dead Sea Scrolls. The manuscripts which were discovered in 1947 and 1948 in various caves in the area of Qumran, on the north-western shore of the Dead Sea,were published at the time. The other manuscripts which were found after the Israel Independence war, however, had still not been published. The Jordanian Archeological Authorities which were now responsible for them, had entrusted these ancient documents to the scholars of the *Ecole Biblique* of the Dominican order in East Jerusalem, which was also under Jordanian rule at the time. They had promised to publish the manuscripts as soon as possible, but forty years had already elapsed and, except for a few fragments, they had not yet done so.

Knowing that a set of copies of the documents had been sent to the Huntington Library in Pasadena, California, for safekeeping purposes, Professor Robert Eisenman approached the curator of the library and requested permission to look at them. His request was granted and he was led to a separate room where he was able to examine the copies of these unique manuscripts. Since he had a small camera in his pocket, he could not resist the temptation to take pictures of the entire collection of photocopies. A few months later, the copies were published by a private foundation and their publication caused an uproar among the scholars of the Dominican School, who thought they had the exclusive custody of these manuscripts. After the original outrage, however, the anger dissipated and scholars from all over the world were finally able to study these ancient documents. Various theories have been advanced to explain the delay in publishing these manuscripts. The Dominican scholars may have thought erroneously that the publication of these documents might be detrimental to the teachings of the Church. They may also have thought that the large public would eventually forget about them altogether. The delaying tactic, however, did not work and the manuscripts were eventually made available to everyone.

When I told the professor that I had studied the original Dead Sea Scrolls with the late professor Dupont-Sommer who taught at the Sorbonne, in Paris, he invited me to join the California team he had formed in order to translate and annotate these documents, in conjunction with the members of another team of scholars from the School of Oriental Studies of the University of Chicago and I eagerly accepted.

This scholarly endeavor gave a new meaning to my life. Even though I could not dedicate myself entirely to it because of my congregational duties, I devoted a part of my days to this fascinating work. I would get up at dawn every day to work on the documents. I would analyze the meaning of every word and every expression to make sure I understood the exact meaning of the text. I translated the manuscripts which had been entrusted to me and I submitted my translations and annotations to Professor Eisenman who in turn reviewed the material and incorporated it in the book which he published.

The Dead Sea Scrolls Uncovered came out in 1991. Among the texts I translated was a unique manuscript which contained the essential part of the second paragraph of the daily Amidah recited in all our prayer services. I had found the earliest mention of the belief in the resurrection of the dead and a reference to God as being the *Messiah* who will redeem the righteous and the pious from their detractors. When I brought these facts to the attention of the professor, he was just as excited as I was. Several researchers have since developed the suggestions I made in my notes and published entire books on these topics. The book was re-edited several times and also translated into French.

After five years of service at Temple Beth Shalom, I decided to retire from the pulpit rabbinate and devote myself to my other vocation: logotherapy. The congregation organized a farewell party for me and my wife and published a little booklet as an expression of gratitude for my five years of service.

I then undertook a research project at Cedars-Sinai Medical Center in Los Angeles with the cooperation of Rabbi Dr Levi Meyer, the senior chaplain of the hospital, who held a doctorate in clinical psychology from the University of Southern California. I devised a questionnaire and I interviewed some forty terminally-ill patients in an attempt to find out whether they thought they had fulfilled their vocation in their life-time. I was hoping that this project would help me find a method that would enable young people to discover their vocation early in their lives, so that they might enjoy a measure of moral satisfaction and happiness in fulfilling it.

I began to conduct experiential seminars in logotherapy and to organize my notes with the intention of writing an introduction to that discipline. I completed my manuscript in French because I thought there was a particular need for it. The little book *Une Démarche Thérapeutique, la Logothérapie (a psychotherapeutic process: logotherapy)* was published by a Paris editor in 2006. I also began writing my memoirs of the World War II and the Holocaust period. *Evading the Nazis, the Story of a Hidden Child in Normandy* was published in January 2009.

XIV
ON THE FRENCH RIVIERA

I was still hoping to fulfill my dream of returning to France in my retirement years. I envisioned the possibility of setting up a part-time practice in logotherapy and Jungian analysis and continuing my research in those fields. After considering various options, I thought that the city of Nice, on the French Riviera, would provide the best opportunity for me to realize my dream. In addition to other good reasons, I had a sentimental one for choosing that city. Nice was the place where my mother had met my father. Rosemary was not very happy about the whole project but she reluctantly let me go, hoping that I would soon come back. I spent three months in Nice to get acquainted with the city and the *Provençal* way of life. I met with various psychotherapists in order to find out how satisfied they were with their practice. Their comments were to be expected. Some of them were encouraging and some were fearful that a new colleague - albeit semi-retired - might pull away some of their clients.

"There are more therapists than we need on the French Riviera," they said to me, "why wouldn't you consider opening a practice in the Southwest or the Northwest region?"

Some others would say:

"I just cannot understand why an American would like to settle in France?"

I pursued my exploration of the city and its surroundings. I visited various cultural and artistic centers and talked to people who were not afraid of competition. They were eager to tell me about their experience and their feelings for the region.

I had been given the address of a family I was to contact when I would be in Nice. When I called them, they graciously invited me to their home with other guests to participate in an informal dinner-party. I thought I would not mention the fact that I was a retired rabbi because I was planning to practice psychotherapy and I wanted them to believe that this was my principal vocation. My host, however, had already called his friend in California and learned the truth about my background. As a consequence, I had to acknowledge the fact that I had been a rabbi for some forty years.

A few days before Rosh Hashanah, one of the guests I had met at the home of my new friend, called me and asked me bluntly if I would be prepared to conduct liberal and egalitarian services for the Jewish New Year. I was quite surprised by the request. I wanted to refuse but I couldn't find the courage to do so and I agreed to meet with the interested people. They were the members of a women's association who were eager to be treated with the same respect as men in the synagogue. As there was little time left before the holiday and they did not know what had to be done, the entire preparation fell on my laps. I rented a hall in an hotel and I placed a small ad in the leading newspaper. Among the people who responded to the ad, was an intrigued reporter who offered to write an article about the services. The story was published the next day and over hundred people called to indicate that they were planning to attend the services. I prepared a little booklet which contained some of the most important prayers with a French translation and made copies of it. I bought a *Shofar*, a ram's horn, to proclaim the new year in the traditional way. I borrowed a scroll of the Torah from a gentleman who had brought it with him from Tunisia. At the indicated time, some 120 people entered the hall eager to participate in a new type of service where men and women were seated next to each other and many prayers would be said in French. A retired cantor, who was a native of Greece, offered to assist us. The participants were pleased with the new format of the service and their curiosity turned into religious fervor. The first step had been made toward the establishment of a liberal congregation in Nice.

It was not my intention, however, to get involved with all the administrative nitty-gritty that would be required in order to ensure the success of such a project. When I realized that the organizing group wanted to establish a congregation like all the others with a board of administration, elected officers and meetings and more agonizing meetings to discuss minor details, my enthusiasm faded away. The founding members applied for a grant from the World Council of Synagogues to help them establish their congregation. After offering my benevolent services for another two months, I decided to return to the United States to be with my wife and at a reasonable distance from my children.

The members of this group pursued their goal with determination. After an exchange of letters and requests for assistance which were repeated over a period of several years, the World Council of Synagogues and the Association of Men's Clubs finally agreed to adopt the new congregation and support it both morally and financially. A French-speaking rabbi, who had just graduated from the Massorti rabbinical seminary in Jerusalem, was invited to lead the new congregation which adopted the name of *Maayane Or* (the Source of Light.) It became the second Conservative congregation in France.

XV
A MISSION TO THE LEMBA TRIBE

When my wife decided to visit her ailing mother in South Africa, I gladly agreed to accompany her. I used that opportunity to include a visit the members of the Lemba tribe who claim to be descendants of the Judeans of Biblical days. Most of their members resided in the northern part of the country. I wrote to Prof. M.E.R. Mathiva, the president of the Lemba Cultural Association, to let him know that I wanted to visit him in Thohoyandou. He answered that he would glad to welcome me and that he would introduce me to some of the leaders of his association.

Once in Johannesburg, I made plans to take a collective taxi in an area of the city which is essentially a black neighborhood. My sister-in-law called the nearby police station and asked if it was safe to go there. To alleviate our concerns, they offered to take me to the taxi terminal in a patrol car. On the appointed day, two policemen accompanied me to a crowded area of the city which is used as the dispatch center for the buses and taxis going in virtually all directions. They found a collective taxi going to Thohoyandou, the capital of the Northern province. They spoke to the driver and asked him to take good care of me. I paid my fare and got into a mini-van which was not only filled with people but with suitcases and all kinds of packages piled up on the knees of the passengers. After a drive that lasted five and a half hours, I arrived at the bus station of Thohoyandou, which is situated near the Limpopo river which serves as the dividing line with Zimbabwe. When I came out of the taxi, I realized I was the only white person on this large plaza. A cousin of the professor, who was the super-intendant of the school district of the region, came to call for me. He first took me to his office and introduced me to his associates and his staff. We then drove to the residence of Prof. Mathiva who had taught African linguistics until his retirement. He was the elected president of the Lemba Cultural Association. The professor graciously invited me to stay at his house for Shabbat and I gladly accepted the honor.

We had an informal conversation which lasted several hours, during which I learned about the aspirations of the Lemba leadership. The Lemba formed an ethnic group of some one hundred thousand or more African natives who resided in three contiguous countries: South Africa, Zimbabwe and Mozambique. They believed they were one of the lost tribes of Israel.

I delivered the laptop computers which had been donated to them by Sandy Leeder, a committed member of Kulanu, an outreach organization, residing in California. I also offered them the books and other publications I had brought with me which were destined for the library of the future Lemba Cultural Center and Synagogue which were under construction.

Around six o'clock, people started coming for the Sabbath eve service, which was held in the living room of the professor's house. Dr Mathiva invited me to conduct the service but I declined because I was not familiar with the Lemba tradition. I agreed to participate only after the professor had completed his part of the service. He then knelt in front of the fireplace on which stood a *Hanukiah*, a candelabrum used during the celebration of Hanukah and several pictures of his children's graduation from university. He said a long prayer in Venda, the vernacular of most of the participants, during which he invoked *Jehovah* and asked for His blessing upon us. He then asked several young participants to read passages from the Torah, including chapter 20 of Exodus, which contains the Ten Commandments, from the translation of a Christian Bible in Venda, the only available in that language. Then the professor asked the young people in the group to sing several hymns - from a Lutheran hymnal - which did not contain any reference to Jesus or the Trinity. They were beautifully sung in perfect harmony and I assumed that the singers had been trained to sing in a choir. When my turn came, I told my audience how glad I was to share this prayer service with my brethren of the Northern province, I gave a study-sermon on the Ten Commandments, told them a few Hassidic stories and taught them some Shabbat traditional songs.

The same type of service took place the next morning, but something entirely unexpected happened immediately after the service was over. Several participants asked me if I would kindly answer a few questions about the Jewish religion and a lively discussion ensued. The questions they asked me were the very same that were raised in many Judeo-Christian interfaith dialogues in other parts of the world. "Can you tell us what the position of Judaism is on original sin, on heaven and hell, forgiveness of sin, the devil and salvation through the sacrifice of Jesus on the cross?" They wanted to know what was the difference between the Christian teachings they had been taught in the Catholic and Lutheran churches they were attending and Judaism. I knew that the first schools for children in this remote area had been established by European missionaries. They had required that the children be baptized in order to be registered as pupils and they had later made the same request of their parents. If the family failed to attend a Sunday religious service without a legitimate excuse, the children risked expulsion from their school.

The Lemba were taught that Christianity represented the "highest form of the Jewish religion" and most of them accepted these teachings and soon became faithful Christians. Hundred twenty years later, some of them were determined to recapture their Jewish heritage and affirm their allegiance to Judaism. They had come to question some of the doctrines which had been imparted to them from childhood on and they were searching the truth in new directions.

I entertained a dialogue by e-mail with a number of them but I realized it was virtually impossible to undo years of indoctrination in a few messages. Even though their intention was to return to Judaism, they were not well equipped to question what their priests and ministers had laboriously taught them in the last four generations. One of the sons of the professor, Dr. Gedzu Mathiva, who practiced medicine in Thohoyandou, had a different view on this whole matter. He was fortunate to have enjoyed a personal acquaintance with members of the American Jewish community during the year he had spent at Harvard University while studying public health after he graduated from Medical School. He told me that his closest friends at Harvard were mainly Jews, that they did not manifest any sign of racism toward him and that he could conceive the idea of being part of the Jewish community. The apartheid regime would have made it impossible for him to develop this kind of friendship.

The professor was also blessed with three daughters. Dr. Rudo (Ahavah) was a Pediatric Intensive Care physician at the Baragwanath Hospital, the medical center of Soweto, the most important hospital of the country and possibly the African continent. She was enrolled at the time in an Introduction to Judaism class which was sponsored by the Orthodox rabbinate of Johannesburg. She had established a friendly relationship with Rabbi Bernhard of the prestigious Oxford Road Synagogue in Killarney. Another daughter was a cardiologist in Durban and a third one was a librarian in Johannesburg. When the professor told me that three of his children were doctors, I spontaneously said to him:

"This alone, Professor, would surely qualify you as a member of the Jewish people."

One of the assistants to the professor was Rabson Wuriga, a nice man in his late thirties, rather shy and unassuming, who was a doctoral candidate in philosophy at the University of Natal in Durban. He had studied Christian theology for several years before he decided to change the course of his studies. I thought he might engage in the study of Jewish theology and philosophy if he had been able to receive a scholarship. One evening, the professor invited Mr Samuel Moetti, the governor of the Thohoyandou area and a former member of the South African Parliament. His main concern was to find ways of creating jobs for the unemployed who were suffering from poverty and hunger. Even though I was not an economist or a specialist in the field of urban development, he thought that I might have some valuable ideas which might help him in his work. Since I belonged to the Jewish community that had produced so many fine economists and businessmen, he probably assumed that I possessed some of the know-how with which many Jews had distinguished themselves in South Africa. He must have thought that I would be able to suggest the right solutions to his problems. We had a long discussion in a most cordial atmosphere.

During my short stay in the Northern province, I also had the opportunity to spend two days with Ephraim Selamolela, a Bhuba (priest among the Lembas) who was recovering from a minor stroke. He was a very successful businessman who owned a large farm in the country, a shopping center in the city and was in the process of finishing the construction of two lodges (30 rooms and rondavels each) on two different sites. The Bhuba Lodge where I stayed, had lovely surroundings, with domesticated and wild animals roaming all over. Ephraim had warned me to be careful if I went down to the river because he had seen a crocodile there a few weeks before.

Ephraim was an interesting character. When he was nine years old, his teacher had called his parents to inform them that their son was not able to keep up with the class and that he should go to work on a farm rather than waste his time sitting in a classroom. The parents, who trusted the judgement of the teacher, took him out of school and sent him to work in the country. In spite of his limited schooling, however, Ephraim turned out to be the most gifted entrepreneur in the entire Lemba community. Even though his teacher had discouraged him from pursuing regular studies, Ephraim made a special effort to acquire some of the knowledge he had not received at school. To my great surprise, I discovered that he was one of the few people, possibly the only person in this remote corner of the world, to own a complete set of the Encyclopedia Britannica. Even though he never attended an architectural school in his life, he himself designed the lodges and stores he built in the country and the city.

Ephraim told me the history of his family and explained to me many of the customs of the Lemba tribe. When he showed me a picture of his father, he told me in a very touching way:

"You see, Rabbi, that is the picture of my father; he looks like a real Jew with fine Semitic features. I look like the African ancestors in my mother's family but, on the other hand, I inherited the intelligence of my father."

"Ephraim," I said, "you are a role model for this community. We are all proud of you."

The Bhubas are the only members of the tribe allowed to slaughter animals for human consumption as do the Shoh'etim (ritual slaughterers) in traditional Jewish communities. Ephraim, the Bhuba, knew all about the slaughtering of animals. Without realizing it, he even told me, one day, the secret prayer which is recited before they proceed with the actual slaughtering of an animal. They say in some ancient African language: "in the name of the all-compassionate and merciful God" which is precisely the prayer recited by the adherents of Islam as they are about to slaughter an animal. The Lemba never eat pork or any animal that resembles the pig like the hippopotamus. They practice circumcision on their male children - and not on their female children as is done in some African tribes - when the boy has reached the age of eleven or twelve and not when the baby is eight days old as the Torah commands. One cannot help noticing that this is the age of circumcision that is prescribed by the teachings of Islam. I soon came to ask myself what these amazing coincidences with Islamic tradition might suggest and I came to the conclusion that the religion and way of life of the Lemba had probably been deeply influenced by Muslim practice at one time or another in the course of their history.

A professor in the department of Old Testament and Ancient Near Eastern Studies at the University of South Africa, Prof. Magdel Le Roux, who wrote her doctoral thesis on the origins of the Lemba ethnic group, reported the hypothesis which had been suggested by some scholars that Christian missionaries may have inadvertently communicated to the Lemba the idea that they might have Jewish origins. Indeed, when they emphatically stated that they would not eat pork meat under any circumstance and that they would continue to circumcise their male children, the missionaries, who were trying to dissuade them from observing these practices, would have said to them:

"The apostle St Paul taught us that we do not have to follow the precepts of the law of Moses anymore. Why do you insist, then, on continuing to emulate the customs of the Hebrews of the Old Testament?"

These words must have made an impact on the new converts to Christianity and they reinforced the belief of some of them that they were descendants of the Hebrews of the Old Testament. The thesis of Prof. Magdel le Roux was published in 2003 under the title "The Lemba, A Lost Tribe of Israel in Southern Africa?" and it was prefaced by Prof. M. L. Daneel, Professor Extraordinary: UNISA, Pretoria and Professor of Missiology at Boston University, School of Theology.

Nearly all the Lemba converted to Christianity; some joined the Catholic church and some the Lutheran church. As they began to read the Bible, many identified with the Hebrews of the Old Testament and were determined to emulate them. This conviction acquired a new significance after the government of the State of Israel undertook the extraordinary rescue of the Ethiopian Jews (Operation Moses) at a time when their country was suffering from a terrible famine. A Lemba Professor of Engineering, who visited Israel a few years later, told me his amazement when he observed how the members of the Beta Israel (Falashas) of Ethiopia had been integrated in the population after some difficulties. They could be seen in all walks of life, serving as officers and soldiers in the army, working as nurses in hospitals and their children studying in schools and religious institutions everywhere. Coming from South Africa where the apartheid regime was strongly in place, the situation he had observed in Israel was like a dream, the fulfillment of the hope his people had entertained for many years.

They welcomed me with great warmth and kindness; they felt honored to have a European-born American rabbi visit them when none of the South African rabbis had expressed the desire to do so. They were particularly touched that I accepted them as brothers and sisters in the process of returning to their ancestral faith. After this first visit, I returned twice to the Northern province to assist the Lemba in their attempt to re-learn or just learn the essential teachings of Judaism.

On my second visit, I arranged for Rabbi Hillel Avidan, my successor at Temple David in Sandton, Sandy Leeder from California and Geoffrey Horwitz, a friend from Johannesburg to come along with me to assist me during our seminar on Judaism. We were given a warm reception by Rabson Wuriga, Dr Gedzu Mathiva, several other tribal elders and our host Ephraim Selamolela.

They were exceedingly grateful to us for visiting them after many years of failure to generate any meaningful interest from the South African Orthodox Jewish community. When Sandy Leeder blew the Shofar for them, one of the elders was very moved and said almost with tears in his eyes,

"This call reminded of my grandfather when he was blowing from his own ram's horn on special occasions."

The attendance was not as good as I had been led to believe, however, and the number of participants diminished after the first day. The fact that I was not teaching in Venda, their mother tongue, was a problem for most of them. No attempt was made for a translator to summarize what I was saying. In addition, I got the feeling that they were just not inclined to study texts and explore new approaches to religious life. They had little knowledge of the teachings of the great prophets like Isaiah or Jeremiah and very little interest in the interpretations of the Talmudic Sages who formulated the guiding principles of modern Judaism. They were frustrated by the fact that the Judaism I was describing to them was not another form of Christianity but a different religion altogether. As a consequence, I began to question the sincerity of their desire to return to the religion of their ancestors as their leaders had communicated it to me.

Still I decided to accept another invitation to conduct a seminar in the Northern Province which was made possible with a small grant from the Kulanu organization. On this visit, however, I was surprised to find out that several Christian professors had been invited to attend the seminar without my being informed. They were Prof. Magdel le Roux of the University of South Africa; her husband who was a minister of the Lutheran Church; Prof. Tudor Parfitt, who taught Modern Jewish Studies at the University of London's School of Oriental and African Studies (SOAS) who had been raised in the Baptist church and Edith Bruder, one of his doctoral students.

I arrived on a Friday afternoon in order to celebrate Shabbat with my new friends at the Bhuba Lodge and conduct a seminar for some hundred fifty participants. The young people who were supposed to attend the week-end seminar did not arrive until late at night. I had planned to teach the thirteen principles of the Jewish faith as they were codified by Maimonides (1135-1204). Since we could not wait for the young people to arrive, I began my first session without them. And then a most regrettable incident took place. As I was about to tell the participants some of the differences that exist between Judaism and Christianity, Prof. Le Roux interrupted my lecture and declared that the participants were not ready for this kind of a lesson. She was determined to protect the Christian faith of these reluctant converts who had invited me specifically to initiate them to Judaism. After this incident, I began to understand the extent of the pressure that was exercised by the missionaries upon their converts to make sure that they would not deviate from the faith they had inculcated in them. The professor never apologized to me for her disruption of my lecture. This incident had happened in the same way the Inquisitors used to harass the Jewish community in the Middle Ages. I was extremely upset and could barely sleep that night. The organizer explained to me a few years later, that these had been the conditions which the black community had to endure under the rule of the white government and especially during the apartheid regime. The Lutheran church had invested a great deal of effort and money in the African populations they had evangelized on the continent of Africa and they had a vested interest in protecting their gains. At this time, however, I began to have serious doubts about the declarations of the organizer who claimed that the Lemba were sincerely considering returning to Judaism.

The buses arrived late at night; the youngsters were exhausted and they went to bed immediately after their arrival. The next morning as I was looking for them to have breakfast with them, they were nowhere to be found and the staff would not answer my questions. I decided to explore the various buildings of the lodge and I eventually found them having a seminar of their own with the official chaplain of the Lemba association who was a staunch believer in the Catholic faith. He was in the process of undoing what I was trying to do. I felt betrayed by the organizer who had invited me to give a seminar in which I would teach the participants the difference between Judaism and Christianity. I regretted having made such a long journey to come to South Africa to teach Judaism to people who had no interest in the Jewish religion.

When I asked the organizer to give me an explanation for this awkward situation, he told me that the elected chaplain of the Lemba association did not share the goals of some of the other leaders of the tribe and that he had been asked by the church to look after the young Lemba to make sure that they would not leave the fold.

He had thus come to this seminar with the sole purpose of counteracting my endeavors. I then realized that the Lemba leaders were divided on the matter of returning to the Jewish religion and that some of them were actually boycotting my seminar. They were so entrenched in their Christian practice that they could not or would not consider changing their religion. That explained also why a *dominee* (pastor) of the Lutheran Church and two Christian professors and a photographer and a reporter for an Afrikaans newspaper had insisted on coming to that seminar as 'observers' in order to intimidate me from pursuing the task I had been asked to fulfill. My coming, however, must have had some beneficial consequences for the Lemba in that the Catholic and the Lutheran churches would now raise their financial assistance to the Lemba community to make sure that they would not defect from their respective churches.

Various hypotheses have been advanced by anthropologists and experts in the field of African studies to explain the eventual connection of the Lemba to the Jewish people in the absence of any written document or archeological data which would give validity to the Lemba claim. Prof. Tudor Parfitt, of the University of London, published several books on the Jews of Africa and the subtitle of one of them suggests what many scholars have been guessing for a long time. The name of the book is quite emphatic "The Lost Tribes of Africa, the History of a Myth." He tried to find some traces of a Lemba presence in the ancient city of Sena in southern Yemen but nothing so far has led to any conclusion. The same professor is convinced that he found some traces of the Ark of the Covenant and he published another book about it. These books make for interesting reading and certainly contribute to broaden the scope of the myth of the ten lost tribes. Reading the account of Tudor Parfitt's adventurous investigations in Africa and the southern part of the Arabian peninsula leaves one with the feeling that he is attempting to emulate Indiana Jones.

He almost succeeded in proving the Jewish origin of the Lemba tribe by using the genetic method of analysis of the DNA. Indeed, the Cohen Modal Haplotype (CMH) or Y chromosome, which was believed at first to be a distinctive marker of the Cohanim (Jewish priests), was also present among the Bhubas. However, further research by Israeli geneticists has shown that the same genetic marker was also found in other ethnic groups like the Kurds, Armenians, some Arabs, Turks, Greeks and Italians. One may thus assume that the CMH is a Mediterranean genetic characteristic and not exclusively Jewish feature. This finding would thus indicate that the Lemba may have some Mediterranean or Middle Eastern ancestry but does not prove in itself that they are descendants of Jews. I also became convinced that the Islamic influence had played a considerable role in their past history before the majority of them eventually converted to Christianity.

It was an amazing experience even though it did not achieve its intended goal. The Lemba will have to decide for themselves whether they really want to become Jews. Their unsubstantiated claim that they are descendants of the Judeans of Biblical days will not change the fact that they are members of Christian churches today. The dream of Professor Mathiva has not been realized but a new charismatic leader may be able, one day, to lead his people to adopt the Jewish faith.

XVI

IN THE LAND OF CACTI

With the purpose of getting closer to my two children who lived in Phoenix, my wife and I decided to retire in Arizona. In order to assist a small congregation, I agreed to serve as the spiritual guide of Congregation Bet Shalom of Tucson. It comprised some sixty families and single people. The members held their services in the extension of a private house they had acquired a few years before and they had installed some prefabricated offices to serve as a religious school.

When I first met with the committee of the congregation, they let me know that several lay members were conducting the Saturday services and that they did not want to change the format they had devised. The president, who had a lovely voice, usually acted as the cantor for the main part of the service. When it came to the Torah reading, they would take out a scroll from the ark and a retired professor would lead the procession. They would then open the scroll on the pulpit and call seven people to the Torah as is customary in most Conservative congregations. One of the participants, standing on the right side of the pulpit, would laboriously read the passage in Hebrew from a printed Pentateuch and another volunteer would follow the reading in the scroll with a pointer. When I offered to read from the scroll, they told me that the members of the congregation were used to this unconventional way of reading the Torah and they did not feel any need to change it. After many conversations over the next few months, I was finally allowed to read from the Torah scroll.

Following the service, we would have a Kiddush in what had been the living room of this old house and then, Elisabeth Greenberg, a vice-president of the congregation, would conduct a study session based either on the Torah reading of the week or a topic of her choice and I was allowed to intervene in the discussion as was every other member of the group. The congregation did not hold a Friday night service except on special occasions. The board of directors seemed to be satisfied with the routine they had developed.

In order to have an opportunity to teach and reach out to potential new members, I organized a Bible class once a week in the meeting room of a Kosher-style cafeteria which was located some six or seven miles away. We soon welcomed an average of thirty participants regularly, of whom a number were members of the congregation and others were not. Elisabeth Goldberg would honor me with her presence.

We had a religious school that comprised some thirty five children. The teachers were paid university students or volunteers who had little knowledge of Judaism. When I offered to teach a different class every evening, the School committee strongly objected for various reasons. In the first place, they had hired the teachers and they felt that the school should continue to be run the way they had done for several years. They asked me to substitute when a teacher was absent but the idea of creating an effective program of religious education was not on the agenda of the committee.

One of the teachers was a student who was going through an intense religious crisis. Yaniv was under the influence of several of his university classmates who were pressuring him to convert to Christianity. He would often ask me to help him find the proper arguments which would enable him to refute the claims of his proselytizing friends. We had many conversations and we exchanged e-mails in the course of the year. I eventually lost contact with him after I retired for the second time. A few years later, however, as I was visiting my youngest son in a Yeshivah for English speaking young men in Jerusalem, I was surprised to meet Yaniv among the students. He had interrupted his university studies to consecrate an entire year to the study of Torah and Talmud. He confessed to me that the discussions we had in Tucson, had played a significant role in his decision to pursue his study of Judaism in Jerusalem.

In spite of the objections of the School committee, I eventually organized a new program for youngsters who were twelve years old and more and who had never studied the Jewish religion before. The students were required to attend a Sunday morning class with at least one of their parents. This approach was meant to offer family education rather than prepare teenagers to recite a few texts in a ceremony marking their coming of age according to Jewish tradition. The class proved to be extremely successful and was well attended. It enabled a dozen youngsters and their parents to acquire a solid background in the basic principles and practices of the Jewish religion. Most of them celebrated their Bar or Bat Mitzvah in the months which followed the completion of this course and all these families joined the congregation in order to do so.

One Saturday morning, I encountered a problem I never had in all the years of my career. An officer of the congregation interrupted me in the middle of a sermon, accusing me of using the pulpit to endorse a candidate who was running for an office. It happened when Senator Joseph Lieberman was chosen to be the running mate of vice-president Al Gore by the democratic party convention which had just taken place. Most Jewish leaders had expressed their satisfaction for the fact that an observant Jewish politician had been chosen as a candidate for such a high office in the United States. I was quoting from a public address of Senator Lieberman in which he stated, "I can only be myself... My religion is important to me. I try my best to be faithful to it and I am strengthened by it."

At that moment, retired Professor Harry Lawrence, a board member of the congregation, stated with a loud and angry voice, that I had no right to endorse a candidate from the pulpit. I responded that it was not my intention to do so. I was only referring to the fact that the American Jewish community had come of age and that even a practicing Orthodox Senator could be running for the vice-presidency of the United States. While most Jews in the country regarded this nomination as a great achievement, some Jews, like my board member, felt ill at ease. They were probably afraid that the election of a Jewish candidate to such a high office might trigger a wave of anti-semitism. Jews should keep a low profile, they thought, in order to appease the anti-Semites who always claim that Jews have too much power in America. I was only conveying the social significance of such a fact and was in no way endorsing a candidate, but the retired professor, who was a staunch Republican, understood my comments differently. I concluded my sermon by reading a passage from an article in the New York Times which quoted from another address of Senator Lieberman to the members of a Black church near Detroit in which he was quoted as saying: "I hope that my commitment to my religion will enable all people to talk about their faith and about their religion, and I hope it will reinforce a belief that I feel as strongly as anything else - that there must be a place for faith in America's public life."

Given the fact that the senator was speaking in a church, his words seemed perfectly appropriate. As Martin E. Marty, the dean of American historians of religion, wrote at the time: "Non-evangelical Americans do not fear that Orthodox Jews will try to convert them, or impose their beliefs on the nation."

My comments were focused on the sociological significance of this new development in the American community and not on the political impact it might have on the electorate. I thought it was my duty as a rabbi to mention this fact without being accused of meddling into politics. I was extremely offended by the intemperate behavior of this board member and I was tempted to announce my resignation right at that moment. I hesitated to do so only because it might be a disservice to some of the other members of the group and especially those who had joined the congregation because of my presence.

For the High Holidays, the congregation used to rent the main hall of the near-by Jewish Community Center and we attracted a large number of non-members who were required to buy tickets in order to attend services. The members of the board were busy checking the names of the people entering the hall to make sure they had paid their dues or had tickets before they could enter to pray.

I was able to convince some thirty five new families and individuals to join the congregation. I waited a few more months and I let the president know that I wanted to resign from my post. The board members accepted my decision and the congregation continued to follow its own tradition without a rabbi.

Several months later, I was surprised to learn that the newly elected president of the congregation had also resigned and had become a member of Congregation Anshei Israel where we often met after Shabbat services.

I began to do all the things I never had a chance to do before. I taught a class in the continuing education program of the University of Arizona and another class at Temple Emanuel, the leading Reform congregation in Tucson. I counseled a few patients who used to come to my home and I began to organized my notes on the various topics of psychotherapy I had written in the course of my career.

As I was reading the Jewish News of the Greater Phoenix, I saw a notice stating that the rabbi of the Sun City West congregation, a retirement community situated in the West Valley of Phoenix, had died suddenly after just a few weeks on the job and only six weeks before the High Holidays. I spontaneously called the congregation and ask them if they needed a rabbi for the approaching holidays. A few days later, a small delegation made up of the president and two members of the board came to Tucson to meet with me in the cafeteria of the Jewish Community Center. We had a nice conversation and they invited me to spend the following week-end in Sun City West. I was to conduct services and preach a sermon on Friday night and Saturday morning in order to get acquainted with the members of the congregation.

Everything went according to plan. The board directors invited me to officiate for the High Holidays and then they asked me if I would consider accepting the post on a permanent basis. My wife and I agreed to make the move. We sold our house in Tucson and we bought a condominium in Sun City West close to the synagogue.

Temple Beth Emeth was essentially a congregation of retirees. Most of their members were from the East Coast or the Midwest. Some lived in Arizona all year long but half of them were "snow-birds" and only spent the winter season in the Western state. The synagogue building had been carefully designed by Max Gimpel, a member of the congregation, who had created virtually everything from the inscriptions on the ark to the stained glass windows representing the twelve tribes of Israel. The congregation was affiliated with the United Synagogue of Conservative Judaism though none of the members had ever attended a regional or national conference.

The congregation endeavored to serve the religious needs of a varied group of members who had received different religious upbringings. On weekdays, the morning service was conducted according to the Orthodox ritual and the participants used a traditional Art Scroll prayer book. On Friday night, the service approximated that of the Reform movement and included a few English readings. On Saturday morning, it was conducted entirely in Hebrew, except for the prayers for the welfare of the nation and the State of Israel and the prayer preceding the recitation of the Mourners Kaddish which included the names of the deceased members of the congregation whose Yahrzeit (anniversary of the death) would occur during the following week. It was a traditional service except for the fact that only one third of the weekly Torah portion was read, as is done in many Conservative congregations.

The members of the Ritual Committee all had an Orthodox background and were quite reluctant to allow any change to take place. Only three or four members could chant the Haftarah (prophetic reading) in Hebrew and they would alternate one Sabbath after another. The committee did not consider the request made by some members of the congregation to allow the Haftarah to be read in an English translation so that all could understand it.

With respect to the observance of the Sabbath, the congregation was following the main stream Conservative approach. Only one gentleman walked to the synagogue on the Sabbath when the weather permitted. Concerning the dietary laws, the members followed their own inclination, but the kitchen of the synagogue was kept Kosher. A dozen families bought meat from a Kosher butcher who delivered their orders on a regular basis. Most of them, however, would often eat in non-Kosher restaurants. This practice enabled them to say that they kept a *Kosher home*.

On Passover, the congregation would hire the services of a Jewish caterer who came from Iowa with a crew of servers in uniforms. The members would read passages of the Haggadah (Passover story) in English or in Hebrew. After the traditional dinner which always included *gefilte* fish and baked chicken, a good number of the participants would leave before we began the second part of the Haggadah.

When I first arrived in Sun City West, the vice president of the congregation who later became president, decided that it would not be a good policy to let the community know that I had been ordained at a Reform seminary. He was the former officer of an Orthodox Synagogue and he thought that the congregation should take a distance from the liberal approach to Judaism. As a result, most of the families that had belonged to a Reform congregation before they settled in our area, would affiliate with the Reform congregation in near-by Sun City.

In the twenty years of its existence, four religious leaders had served Temple Beth Emeth. The first one was a Conservative rabbi who had just retired in Sun City West and who volunteered his services until he died. He was followed by three Orthodox rabbis because the Rabbinical Assembly was unable to provide the congregation with a suitable rabbi for the post. Many of the members had a vivid nostalgia of the Orthodox tradition they had known in their childhood. The Ritual Committee would therefore hire a traditional cantor for the High Holidays who sang the liturgy in the old musical tradition of the Eastern-European communities.

There were actually three groups of members within the congregation. There were those who attended only Friday night services, those who came only on Saturday mornings and those who never came except on the High Holidays. Some of them had joined the congregation to make sure that a rabbi would officiate at their funeral when the time came. There were only half a dozen members who attended both the Friday night and the Saturday morning services.

The members of the congregation were particularly appreciative of the pastoral visits I made to them when they were hospitalized or were recovering in a rehabilitation center or their private home. They would often say to me,

"I am so glad you came to visit me. My neighbor has already had two visits from his minister and I was just wondering whether my rabbi would come to see me too."

The president of the congregation not only chaired the board of directors but also assumed the task of executive director. He would spend most mornings in his office at the synagogue to take care of all the administrative matters. As a consequence, we had many opportunities to consult with each other on every important issue. I enjoyed a fine cooperation with two successive presidents. The third president was an ambitious man, more inclined to give orders than to work with the rabbi. When I suggested that we adopt a new High Holiday prayer-book, because the one we were using had become obsolete, he refused to call the regional office of the Conservative movement to find out about the possibility of getting new or used prayer-books. His primary allegiance was to the Orthodox movement and not to the Conservative one. He thought that the old High Holiday prayer-books were adequate and that there was no urgent need to adopt new ones. He was an able administrator but he was not particularly concerned about the meaning of services as long as the proper Hebrew texts were recited with or without understanding. That was the way he had been brought up.

In spite of that, the adult education classes were very well attended. I gave several series of lectures which attracted between eighty and hundred members and non-members. The classes had to be held in the main sanctuary because no other room could accommodate such a large crowd. My students were more interested in learning about the great ideas of the biblical prophets than practicing all the details of Jewish law. I thought more than once that we should replace our regular worship service with an inter-active Jewish civilization class. We would have a better attendance at our Sabbath religious gatherings. Some prominent rabbis had actually advocated that we institute a study-service to replace the prayer-service which was suffering from attrition. Many members of the congregation, however, were fearful of any change. and did not want to depart from the ways of their youth. They believed in continuity and faithfulness to the tradition of the past with its melodies and long moments of silence until everyone would stand up to recite a few words. The repetition was part of the routine and soothing to many of them. "Why change?" they would say, "that is the way I have always felt in the synagogue."

It did not matter whether you understood the traditional prayers in Hebrew or did not. The important thing was that you were there when the rabbi prayed on behalf of the congregation. Attendance at a Sabbath worship had become the sacred ritual one had to fulfill in order to deserve the divine blessing of life and health. My main problem was that I was not old enough to understand this way of looking at religion.

Two weeks before Passover, at the suggestion of the chairman of the Adult Education Committee, I planned to have a study session immediately after the Sabbath morning service which would focus on the special preparation for the holiday. In order to allocate enough time for this session, it was agreed with the Ritual Committee that I would abbreviate some of the prayers. I let the worshippers know right at the beginning of the service that some passages would be omitted on that day. When I skipped a few psalms and prayers, however, some of the old-timers sitting in the pews got very upset and manifested their discontent in loud voices. The president came down from the podium and went to talk with the various individuals who were complaining. I could not concentrate in the service with all the tumult which followed. The sanctuary had become a parlor where many were wondering why the rabbi had taken upon himself to shorten the service. They were not aware of the fact that it had been agreed beforehand with the members of the proper committees and that I had made an announcement at the start of the service because they were probably not there at the time.

I was tempted to leave the synagogue at that very moment. In consideration for those who had come especially for the study session, however, I completed the service and I conducted my seminar on the meaning of Passover. Inside my heart, however, I had made the decision to resign from my post. The chairman of the adult education committee understood what had happened and she expressed her sympathy to me, but no one else realized how hurt I was by this lack of reverence. I heard a board member say: "It was all the rabbi's idea." In other terms, it was the rabbi's fault and everyone knows that you can always blame the rabbi for everything in the synagogue. Within the next few weeks, I offered to resign from my post. The president and the members of the board of directors did not even care to know my reasons. I insisted on telling them why I had been frustrated but the facts I was mentioning were not of interest to them. They accepted my resignation and we parted ways in a most unfriendly fashion.

Two years later, a Reform congregation was established in Sun City West which meets a few blocks away from the Conservative congregation and it is already attracting more worshippers on Friday nights than Congregation Beth Emeth. And then another Conservative group planned to start its activities.

XVII

A MISSION TO THE CRYPTO-JEWS OF

PORTUGAL

When Rufina Bernardetti Mausenbaum, the president of *Saudades,* the leading outreach organization to the descendants of the Crypto-Jews of Portugal, informed us that she was organizing a tour to the historical sites of Jewish interest in the country of her ancestors, my wife and I gladly signed up for it. The tour began in Lisbon and took us to some ten different cities and villages where our brethren had prospered until the fateful year 1497. Barely five years after the Jews of neighboring Spain were expelled, King Manuel had decreed that all the Jews of Portugal were to be expelled unless they converted to Catholicism. Between hundred thirty and hundred fifty thousand Jews gathered in the major ports from which they expected to leave the country, when King Manuel changed his mind at the last minute and ordered all Jews be be forcibly baptized and remain in the country. Hundreds of priests were summoned to administer the sacraments. They sprinkled holy water over the Jews' heads and they were declared *Cristaos novos* (new Christians) and forbidden to leave the country.

Some of the New Christians managed to clandestinely escape from Portugal in the decades and even century which followed. Most of those who remained in the country, retained some elements of their ancestral tradition for several generations until all that was left was a vague memory of their Judaic origins. Now, five hundred years later, the directors of tourism in these cities, were pleased to welcome us and give us a glorious account of the exceptional contribution made by Jews to their city and their country. They accompanied us to the various neighborhoods where Jews - later new Christians - were allowed to reside, often pointing out the "Street of the Jews" or a house which may have served as a synagogue before the forced conversion of 1497. On several occasions, they showed us the little groove carved in the stone at the entrance door of a specific house which indicated that a Mezuzah had originally been placed in that spot.

When   we visited Coimbra and Evora, we made a point of passing by the palaces of the Inquisition and we stopped in front of them to recite the mourners' Kaddish in memory of the innocent victims who were accused of the crime of *Judaizing* and who perished at the stake in these places. When we entered the buildings believed to have served as synagogues, we sang hymns of the Sephardic tradition. It was a particularly moving experience for all of us to walk in the footsteps of our brethren who had lived and prospered in this country until they were banished and converted against their will.

When we passed by the University of Coimbra, I remembered the distinguished Professor Antonio Homem who had taught Canon Law in one of the classrooms of the institution. So highly regarded was he, that the pope himself would consult him on matters of Canonic law. He was eventually arrested by the agents of the Inquisition and put on trial after his name was mentioned by one of his friends under torture. He was imprisoned in Lisbon for four and a half years before he was relaxed to the civilian authorities who had him burned alive in an *auto-da-fe* which took place in 1624. He was the leader of a group of *Anussim* who used to gather secretly to pray and celebrate the Jewish holidays. In 2008, the University of Coimbra organized an exhibit devoted to the Jewish past of the city and the writings of Antonio Homen were put on display. A notice in small print must have been placed under the exhibited manuscripts stating that their author had been condemned to die in an *auto da fe* by the Tribunal of the Inquisition.

The tour took us later to the village where Aristides de Sousa Mendes was born and where he was buried. He had been the Consul General of Portugal in Bordeaux, France, during World War II. He had single-handedly provided safe-conducts to some thirty thousand Jews by granting them visas which enabled them to leave France and travel to Portugal. He had ignored the orders he received from the central government and had acted deliberately to save human lives. He was eventually suspended from the diplomatic corps and left without any resources.

After his son told us what his father had done during the war, we recited the traditional memorial prayers at his grave and we planted a tree in honor of the man who was instrumental in saving more human lives than any other person except for the Swedish emissary to Hungary, Raoul Wallenberg.

I returned to Portugal on two occasions to conduct seminars for the descendants of the Crypto-Jews who were interested in returning to Judaism. I was instrumental in helping the Lisbon group establish their own congregation which is now functioning under the auspices of *Masorti Olami*, the World Council of Synagogues.

In December 2008, a number of geneticists made public the results of their investigations in the Iberian peninsula. It was widely reported in the New York Times and other specialized publications. They found that over 20% of the residents of Spain were descendants of Jews. These findings would indicate that a larger proportion of the Spanish Jewish community might have converted to Catholicism in 1492 and before than was originally believed. The most amazing revelation, however, concerns the people of Portugal. Whereas 25% of the population of the northern part of the country have Jewish genes in their genetic make-up, 35% of the residents of the southern part of the country have been shown to be descendants of Jews! This makes Portugal the second country after the state of Israel, to have the highest incidence of people of Jewish descent in the world. "O Portugal, the country I love," wrote a Jew who managed to escape clandestinely, "how can I forget thee?"

XVIII
REFUSING TO RETIRE

On my return from Portugal, I pursued my research in the field of existential analysis and stayed away from rabbinical duties until a couple of months before the Jewish new year. I then thought I could make a contribution to my fellow coreligionists who do not belong to an established congregation. Finding creative ways of reaching out to the unaffiliated members of the community had always been one of my ambitions. I first had to understand why many Jews did not join a temple. The scholarly literature on the subject confirmed what I already knew from experience. Some had not found the congregation that was suited to their needs or expectations. Others did not like the rabbi or the board of directors of the congregations they had visited. The majority of them, however, objected to the principle of having to buy high priced tickets in order to attend services on the occasion of the Jewish new year.

I therefore decided to offer free High Holiday services to anyone who might be interested. I rented the Phoenix Unitarian church and borrowed one hundred Orthodox prayer-books and a scroll of the Torah from a colleague who did not plan to conduct services that year. These were the only prayer-books I could find. The Conservative, Reconstructionist and Reform movements refused to lend me old prayer-books because the services I was planning to conduct would be non-denominational. I prepared a little pamphlet which included some of the main prayers and the text of some traditional and modern Jewish songs. I intended to make enough copies for everyone to have his own. I placed a few ads in the Jewish News of Phoenix and was amazed by the results. Over four hundred people called to register for my services. I could accommodate only three hundred because that was the maximum capacity of the venue I had rented. We had lively and short services in an ecumenical spirit. I gave sermons focused on basic human concerns like the search for happiness and peace of mind and told my audience some meaningful stories from the Jewish and universal folklore. I was most gratified with the outcome of these unconventional services and received a number of messages like this one:

"We appreciate what you did for us. It was time for the community to realize that we too belong to the Jewish people. Even though we are not members of a temple or a synagogue, we nevertheless wish to celebrate the Jewish new year and express our allegiance to the Jewish tradition."

"My friends," I answered them, I am glad you participated in our services but I wish to let you know that this undertaking was not a project of any communal or religious organization. It was the expression of my personal desire to serve the community at large. Now that I am retired from the institutional rabbinate, I was in a position to do what I had always wanted to do but was unable to realize because I was employed by a congregation. Temples and synagogues unfortunately, need a lot of revenues to operate their facilities the way they do and as a consequence, they tend to impose a heavy financial burden on their members."

While many of my coreligionists appreciated what I did, most of my colleagues were very unhappy. Several of them let me know that the project I had conducted was a disservice to them. My attempt to reach out to the unaffiliated was luring away some Jewish people from joining their synagogues and become dues-paying members. I explained to them that this argument was nothing but a fallacy because there were eighty thousand Jews in the greater Phoenix who did not belong to any congregation. Three or four hundred of them was just a drop in the bucket. They had not read the many studies written by expert Jewish and Christian demographers who had examined the causes of non-affiliation with a religious congregation. My colleagues seemed to be more concerned about their own financial security than about reaching out to those who were estranged from the synagogue.

Their comments left me undeterred because I knew I was following the right path. Researchers at Brandeis University, the Jewish Outreach Institute and professors at several seminaries had studied this phenomenon and published some enlightening essays on the question.

When the second Lebanese war broke out, I went to Israel to offer my services as a volunteer at the Rambam Hospital in Haifa where many soldiers were recovering from the wounds they had suffered during the fighting. I then moved to Jerusalem to assist the Jewish chaplain at the Shaarey Tzedek Hospital. I would visit the patients and try to speak with them in their native tongue. I knew enough Arabic phrases to befriend the Muslim patients. On occasion, I would recite a verse from the Koran and this would always elicit a big smile because they knew I was a Jew.

My youngest son, Jonathan, was studying in a Yeshivah in Jerusalem at the time. On Fridays, he would volunteer at the H'azon Yeshayah Soup Kitchen in the heart of Jerusalem. I joined him and other volunteers from various countries, including a French Protestant minister. We helped prepare and serve nutritious meals to the hundreds of indigent residents of this religious neighborhood. One Friday, two dozen soldiers in uniform came to work with us. As a consequence, the preparation of the meals was completed in less than an hour. On other Fridays, entire classes of a near-by religious high-school for girls would come to assist in peeling and washing the vegetables for the next meal. Our common desire was to be of assistance to the underprivileged members of the community.

XIX

REFLECTIONS

Vincent van Gogh once said, "I am not an adventurer by choice, but by fate." As for me, I am convinced that I was born to be an adventurer by design and not by accident. The Master of our Destinies must have known this predicament from the very beginning. I discovered it at every turn of my journey through life.

Even though human beings have basically the same needs and the same aspirations to fulfill themselves, they often choose different paths to achieve these goals. During my career in several communities around the world, I have been fascinated by the courage and resilience of my fellows coreligionists wherever they lived. Whether in South Africa or the Caribbean island of Curaçao, I met Jews who were attached to their roots and striving with all their heart to follow the teachings of their faith, in spite of the many obstacles they faced every day. Most of them made a determined effort to resist the constant pressure of the majority to erase all differences and integrate them in their culture and religion.

As for me, these adventures in foreign lands have helped me develop the insight I might never otherwise have attained. I was forced to take the road of the wandering Jew on account of the insensitivity of some clerics but it turned out to be an invaluable experience which made me a better person. I am convinced that Providence must have guided me on my path through life and that it was in these remote places of the world that I was destined to find the God of my Fathers.